CLASSIC SOUPS

CLASSIC SOUPS

MORE THAN 90 DELICIOUS RECIPES FROM AROUND THE
WORLD SHOWN STEP BY STEP IN OVER 400 PHOTOGRAPHS

DEBRA MAYHEW

southwater

This edition is published by Southwater, an imprint of Anness Publishing Limited,
Hermes House, 88–89 Blackfriars Road, London SE1 8HA
tel. 020 7401 2077; fax 020 7633 9499;
www.southwaterbooks.com; www.annesspublishing.com

If you like the images in this book and would like to investigate using them for publishing, promotions or
advertising, please visit our website www.practicalpictures.com for more information.

UK agent: The Manning Partnership Ltd;
tel. 01225 478444; fax 01225 478440; sales@manning-partnership.co.uk
UK distributor: Grantham Book Services Ltd;
tel. 01476 541080; fax 01476 541061; orders@gbs.tbs-ltd.co.uk
North American agent/distributor: National Book Network;
tel. 301 459 3366; fax 301 429 5746; www.nbnbooks.com
Australian agent/distributor: Pan Macmillan Australia;
tel. 1300 135 113; fax 1300 135 103; customer.service@macmillan.com.au
New Zealand agent/distributor: David Bateman Ltd; tel. (09) 415 7664; fax (09) 415 8892

Publisher: Joanna Lorenz; **Managing Editor:** Helen Sudell
Project Editors: Debra Mayhew and Helen Marsh; **Designer:** Bill Mason; **Production Controller:** Pirong Wang
Recipe Contributors: Catherine Atkinson, Alex Barker, Michelle Berriedale-Johnson, Anglela Boggiano,
Janet Brinkworth, Carla Capalbo, Kit Chan, Jacqueline Clark, Maxine Clark, Frances Cleary,
Carole Clements, Andi Clevely, Trish Davies, Roz Denny, Patrizia Diemling, Matthew Drennan,
Sarah Edmonds, Joanna Farrow, Rafi Fernandez, Christine France, Sarah Gates, Shirley Gill,
Rosamund Grant, Rebekah Hassan, Deh-Ta Hsiung, Shehzad Husain, Judy Jackson, Sheila Kimberley,
Masaki Ko, Elisabeth Lambert Ortiz, Ruby Le Bois, Gilly Love, Lesley Mackley, Norma MacMillan,
Sue Maggs, Kathy Man, Sallie Morris, Annie Nichols, Maggie Pannell, Katherine Richmond,
Anne Sheasby, Jenny Stacey, Liz Trigg, Hilaire Walden, Laura Washburn, Steven Wheeler,
Kate Whiteman, Elizabeth Wolf-Cohen, Jeni Wright
Photographers: Karl Adamson, Edward Allwright, David Armstrong, Steve Baxter, James Duncan,
John Freeman, Ian Garlick, Michelle Garrett, Amanda Heywood, Janine Hosegood, David Jordan, William Lingwood,
Patrick McLeary, Michael Michaels, Thomas Odulate, Juliet Piddington, Peter Reilly

ETHICAL TRADING POLICY
Because of our ongoing ecological investment programme, you, as our customer, can have the pleasure
and reassurance of knowing that a tree is being cultivated on your behalf to naturally replace the
materials used to make the book you are holding. For further information about this scheme,
go to www.annesspublishing.com/trees

A CIP catalogue record for this book is available from the British Library.

Previously published as *Great Soup*

NOTES
Bracketed terms are intended for American readers.
For all recipes, quantities are given in both metric and imperial measures and, where appropriate, in standard
cups and spoons. Follow one set of measures, but not a mixture, because they are not interchangeable.
Standard spoon and cup measures are level. 1 tsp = 5ml, 1 tbsp = 15ml, 1 cup = 250ml/8fl oz.
Australian standard tablespoons are 20ml. Australian readers should use 3 tsp in place of 1 tbsp for measuring
small quantities. American pints are 16fl oz/2 cups. American readers should use 20fl oz/2.5 cups in
place of 1 pint when measuring liquids. Electric oven temperatures in this book are for conventional ovens. When using a
fan oven, the temperature will probably need to be reduced by about 10–20°C/20–40°F. Since ovens vary, you should
check with your manufacturer's instruction book for guidance.
Medium (US large) eggs are used unless otherwise stated.

CONTENTS

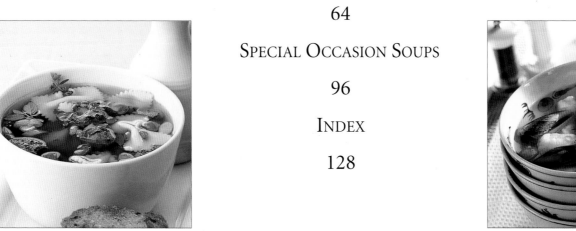

Introduction

Whether you want an elegant first course for a formal dinner party, an easy-to-make, one-pot supper or a light, summery lunch, home-made soup fits the bill and always seems special. Making soup doesn't have to be hard work, especially if you have a blender or food processor to chop vegetables or purée the mixture. Many of the soups in this book require little preparation so once they are cooking, you can get on with something else, while the kitchen fills with an appetizing aroma.

The secret of a really great soup is home-made stock and this is where to begin. Recipes are given for all kinds of stocks, including Chinese and

Japanese. Make them in advance and freeze them in individual recipe portions, so that they are to hand when you are ready to start cooking. The useful introductory section also features some clever ideas for stunning garnishes and easy ways to transform a simple bowl of soup into a dish fit for a king.

The recipes for the soups themselves are divided into four chapters. Light & Refreshing Soups includes cool classics, such as Vichyssoise, as well delicate soups to be served hot, such as Carrot and Coriander. Adventurous cooks – and diners – will enjoy trying the Hot & Spicy Soups inspired by the cuisines of Mexico, India, China,

Thailand, Indonesia and many other countries. Whether based on vegetables, fish, meat or even fruit, they all prove that variety really is the spice of life. Winter Warming Soups will make you positively look forward to the colder months of the year. What could be more comforting and satisfying than a steaming bowl of French Onion Soup or Creamy Cod Chowder while the weather does its worst outside? Special Occasion Soups provides a wonderful opportunity to show off your talents. There are unusual recipe combinations, such as Beetroot Soup with Ravioli, for the experienced cook, as well as equally delicious, but simpler recipes, such as

Pear and Watercress Soup, for those with less time to spare or less cooking confidence.

Extra advice on preparation, freezing and varying the ingredients is provided throughout the book. Key steps of all the recipes are illustrated and the photographs of the finished dishes all look good enough to eat. The V-symbol used throughout the book provides an at-a-glance guide to soups suitable for vegetarians. Some of these contain cheese, but you can substitute vegetarian cheese easily.

Whatever your budget, level of skill, favourite flavours and available time, this book will prove that soup really is great.

Making Your Own Stocks

Fresh stocks are indispensable for creating good home-made soups. They add a depth of flavour that plain water just cannot achieve.

Although many supermarkets now sell tubs of fresh stock, these can be expensive, especially if you need large quantities. Making your own is surprisingly easy and much more economical, particularly if you can use leftovers – the chicken carcass from Sunday lunch, for example, or the shells you're left with once you've peeled prawns (shrimp). But home-made stocks aren't just cheaper, they're also a lot tastier and they're much more nutritious too, precisely because they're made with fresh, natural ingredients.

You can, of course, use stock (bouillon) cubes or granules, but be sure to check the seasoning as these tend to be high in salt.

One good idea for keen and regular soup makers is to freeze home-made stock in plastic freezer bags, or ice cube trays, so you always have a supply at your disposal whenever you need some.

Frozen stock can be stored in the freezer for up to six months. Ensure that you label each stock carefully for easy identification.

Use the appropriate stock for the soup you are making. Onion soup, for example, is improved with a good beef stock. Be particularly careful to use a vegetable stock if you are catering for vegetarians.

Recipes are given on the following pages for vegetable stock, fish stock, meat stock, chicken stock and basic stocks for Chinese and Japanese cooking.

Vegetable Stock

Use this versatile stock as the basis for all vegetarian soups.

INGREDIENTS

Makes 2.5 litres/4½ pints/11 cups

2 leeks, roughly chopped

3 celery sticks, roughly chopped

1 large onion, with skin, chopped

2 pieces fresh root ginger, chopped

1 yellow (bell) pepper, seeded
   and chopped

1 parsnip, chopped

mushroom stalks

tomato peelings

45ml/3 tbsp light soy sauce

3 bay leaves

a bunch of parsley stalks

3 sprigs of fresh thyme

1 sprig of fresh rosemary

10ml/2 tsp salt

freshly ground black pepper

3.5 litres/6 pints/15 cups cold water

1 Put all the ingredients into a very large pan. Bring slowly to the boil, then lower the heat and simmer for 30 minutes, stirring from time to time.

2 Allow to cool. Strain, then discard the vegetables. The stock is ready to use. Alternatively, chill or freeze the stock and keep it to use as required.

Fish Stock

Fish stock is much quicker to make than poultry or meat stock. Ask your fishmonger for heads, bones and trimmings from white fish.

INGREDIENTS

Makes about 1 litre/ 1³/₄ pints/4 cups

675g/1¹/₂lb heads, bones and trimmings from white fish

1 onion, sliced

2 celery sticks with leaves, chopped

1 carrot, sliced

¹/₂ lemon, sliced (optional)

1 bay leaf

a few sprigs of fresh parsley

6 black peppercorns

1.35 litres/2¹/₄ pints/6 cups cold water

150ml/¹/₄ pint/²/₃ cup dry white wine

1 Rinse the fish heads, bones and trimmings well under cold running water. Put in a stockpot with the vegetables and lemon, if using, the herbs, peppercorns, water and wine. Bring to the boil, skimming the surface frequently, then reduce the heat and simmer for 25 minutes.

2 Strain the stock without pressing down on the ingredients in the strainer. If not using immediately, leave to cool and then chill in the refrigerator. Fish stock should be used within 2 days, or it can be frozen for up to 3 months.

Chicken Stock

A good home-made poultry stock is invaluable in the kitchen. If poultry giblets are available, add them (except the livers) with the wings. Once made, chicken stock can be kept in an airtight container in the refrigerator for 3–4 days, or frozen for longer storage (up to 6 months).

INGREDIENTS

Makes about 2.5 litres/4 ½ pints/11 cups

1.2–1.5kg/2½–3lb chicken or turkey
   (wings, backs and necks)
2 onions, unpeeled, quartered
1 tbsp olive oil
4 litres/7 pints/17½ cups cold water
2 carrots, roughly chopped
2 celery sticks, with leaves if possible,
   roughly chopped
a small handful of fresh parsley
a few sprigs of fresh thyme or
   3.5ml/¾ tsp dried thyme
1 or 2 bay leaves
10 black peppercorns, lightly crushed

1 Combine the poultry wings, backs and necks in a stockpot with the onion quarters and the oil. Cook over moderate heat, stirring occasionally, until the poultry and onions are lightly and evenly browned.

2 Add the water and stir well to mix in the sediment on the bottom of the pan. Bring to the boil and skim off the impurities as they rise to the surface of the stock.

3 Add the chopped carrots and celery, fresh parsley, thyme, bay leaf and black peppercorns. Partly cover the stockpot and gently simmer the stock for about 3 hours.

4 Strain the stock through a sieve into a bowl and leave to cool, then chill in the refrigerator for an hour.

5 When cold, carefully remove the layer of fat that will have set on the surface. Store in the refrigerator for 3–4 days or freeze until required.

Meat Stock

The most delicious meat soups rely on a good home-made stock for success. A stock (bouillon) cube will do if you do not have time to make your own. Meat stock can be kept in the refrigerator for 4–5 days, or frozen for longer storage.

INGREDIENTS

Makes about 2 litres/3½ pints/9 cups

1.75kg/4lb beef bones, such as shin, leg, neck and shank, or veal or lamb bones, cut into 6cm/2½in pieces

2 onions, unpeeled, quartered

2 carrots, roughly chopped

2 celery sticks, with leaves if possible, roughly chopped

2 tomatoes, coarsely chopped

4.5 litres/7½ pints/20 cups cold water

a handful of parsley stalks

few sprigs of fresh thyme or 3.5ml/¾ tsp dried thyme

2 bay leaves

10 black peppercorns, lightly crushed

1 Preheat the oven to 230°C/ 450°F/Gas 8. Put the bones in a roasting tin (pan) and roast, turning occasionally, for 30 minutes until they start to brown.

2 Add the onions, carrots, celery and tomatoes and baste with the fat in the tin. Roast for a further 20–30 minutes until the bones are well browned. Stir and baste occasionally.

3 Transfer the bones and roasted vegetables to a stockpot. Spoon off the fat from the roasting tin. Add a little of the water to the roasting tin and bring to the boil on top of the stove, stirring well to scrape up any browned bits. Pour this liquid into the stockpot.

4 Add the remaining water to the pot. Bring just to the boil, skimming frequently to remove all the foam from the surface. Add the parsley, thyme, bay leaves and peppercorns.

5 Partly cover the stockpot and simmer the stock for 4–6 hours. The bones and vegetables should always be covered with liquid, so top up with a little boiling water from time to time if necessary.

6 Strain the stock through a colander, then skim as much fat as possible from the surface. If possible, cool the stock and then chill in the refrigerator; the fat will rise to the top and set in a layer that can be removed easily.

Stock for Chinese Cooking

This stock is an excellent basis for soup making.

INGREDIENTS

Makes 2.5 litres/4¹/₂ pints/11 cups

675g/1¹/₂lb chicken portions

675g/1¹/₂lb pork spare ribs

3.75 litres/6 pints/16 cups cold water

3–4 pieces fresh root ginger, unpeeled, crushed

3–4 spring onions (scallions), each tied into a knot

45–60ml/3–4 tbsp Chinese rice wine

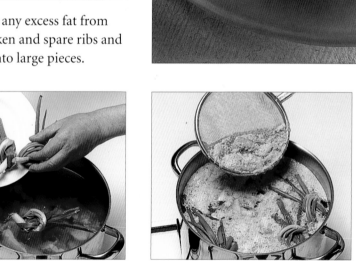

1 Trim off any excess fat from the chicken and spare ribs and chop them into large pieces.

2 Place the chicken and spare rib pieces into a large stockpot with the water. Add the ginger and spring onion knots.

3 Bring to the boil and, using a sieve, skim off the froth. Reduce the heat and simmer, uncovered, for about 2–3 hours.

4 Strain the stock, discarding the chicken, pork, ginger and spring onions. Add the Chinese rice wine and return to the boil. Simmer for 2–3 minutes. Chill the stock in the refrigerator when cool. It will keep for up to 4–5 days. Alternatively, it can be frozen in small containers and thawed when required.

Stock for Japanese Cooking

Dashi is the stock that gives the characteristically Japanese flavour to many dishes. Known as Ichiban-dashi, *it is used for delicately flavoured dishes, including soups. Of course instant stock is available in all Japanese supermarkets, either in granule form, in concentrate or even in a tea-bag style. Follow the instructions on the packet.*

INGREDIENTS

Makes about 800ml/1¹/₃ pints/3¹/₂ cups

10g/¹/₄oz dried kombu seaweed

10–15g/¹/₄–¹/₂oz bonito flakes

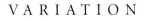

1 Wipe the kombu seaweed with a damp cloth and cut two slits in it with scissors, so that it flavours the stock effectively.

2 Soak the kombu in 900ml/ 1¹/₂ pints/3³/₄ cups cold water for 30–60 minutes.

3 Heat the kombu in its soaking water over a moderate heat. Just before the water boils, remove the seaweed. Then add the bonito flakes and bring to the boil over a high heat, then remove the pan from the heat.

4 Leave the stock until all the bonito flakes have sunk to the bottom of the pan. Line a strainer with kitchen paper or muslin (cheesecloth) and place it over a large mixing bowl, then gently strain the stock.

VARIATION
∾

For vegetarian dashi, just omit the bonito flakes (dried tuna) and follow the same method.

Garnishes

Sometimes, a soup needs something to lift it out of the realms of the ordinary, and garnishes are the answer. They are an important finishing touch, bringing that little extra to soups; they not only look good, but also add an extra dimension to the flavour. A garnish can be as simple as a sprinkling of chopped parsley, a swirl of cream or some freshly grated cheese. Alternatively, it can be something that requires a little more attention, such as home-made croûtons or sippets. All the garnishes here are suitable for vegetarians.

DUMPLINGS

These dumplings are easy to make and add an attractive and tasty finishing touch to country soups.

INGREDIENTS

75g/3oz/½ cup semolina or flour
1 egg, beaten
45ml/3 tbsp milk or water
a generous pinch of salt
15ml/1 tbsp chopped fresh parsley

1 Combine all the ingredients into a soft, elastic dough. Set aside, covered with clear film (plastic wrap), for 5–10 minutes.

2 Drop small rounded dessert-spoonfuls of this mixture into the soup and cook for 10 minutes until firm. Serve immediately.

CRISPY CROÛTONS

Croûtons add a lovely crunchy texture to creamy soups and are a good way of using up stale bread. Use thinly sliced ciabatta or French bread for delicious results.

INGREDIENTS

bread
good quality, flavourless oil, such as sunflower or groundnut (peanut) or, for a fuller flavour, extra virgin olive oil or a flavoured oil such as one with garlic and herbs or chilli

1 Preheat the oven to 200°C/400°F/Gas 6. Cut the bread into small cubes and place on a baking sheet.

2 Brush with your chosen oil, then bake for about 15 minutes until golden and crisp. Allow to start to cool: they crisp up further as they cool down.

3 Store them in an airtight container for up to a week. Reheat in a warm oven, if liked, before serving.

RIVELS

Rivels are pea-size pieces of dough which swell when cooked in a soup.

INGREDIENTS

1 egg
75–115g/3–4oz/¾–1 cup flour
2.5ml/½ tsp salt
freshly ground black pepper

1 Beat the egg in a bowl. Add the flour, salt and pepper to taste and mix with a wooden spoon. Finish mixing with your fingers, rubbing to blend the egg and flour together to form pea-size pieces.

2 Bring the soup to the boil. Sprinkle in the pieces of dough, stirring gently.

3 Reduce the heat and simmer for about 6 minutes, until the rivels are slightly swollen and cooked. Serve immediately.

SWIRLED CREAM

A swirl of cream is the classic finish for many soups, such as a smooth tomato soup or chilled asparagus soup. The garnish gives a professional finish to your soup, although the technique is simplicity itself.

INGREDIENTS

single (light) cream

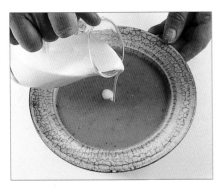

1 Transfer the cream into a jug (pitcher) with a good pouring lip. Pour a swirl on to the surface of each bowl of soup.

2 Draw the tip of a fine skewer quickly backwards and forwards through the cream to create a delicate pattern. Serve the soup immediately.

SIPPETS

Another good way of using up slightly stale bread, sippets are larger than croûtons and have a more intense flavour because of the addition of fresh herbs. Experiment with the herbs according to the flavour of the soup.

INGREDIENTS

3 slices day-old bread

50g/2oz/4 tbsp butter

45ml/3 tbsp finely chopped fresh parsley, or coriander (cilantro) or basil

1 Cut the bread into fingers about 2.5cm/1in long.

2 Melt the butter in a large frying pan, toss in the small fingers of bread and fry gently until golden brown.

3 Add the fresh herbs and stir well to combine. Cook for a further minute, stirring constantly. Strew the sippets on top of the soup and serve.

LEEK HAYSTACKS

Stacks of golden leek look good served on a creamy soup and the crunchy texture contrasts well with the smoothness of the soup.

INGREDIENTS

1 large leek

30ml/2 tbsp plain (all-purpose) flour

oil, for deep-frying

1 Slice the leek in half lengthways and then cut into quarters. Cut into 5cm/2in lengths and then into very fine strips. Place in a bowl, sprinkle the flour over and toss to coat.

2 Heat the oil to 160°C/325°F. Drop small spoonfuls of the floured leeks into the oil and cook for 30–45 seconds until golden. Drain on kitchen paper. Repeat with the remaining leeks.

3 Serve the soup with a small stack of leeks piled on top of each bowl.

LIGHT &
REFRESHING
SOUPS

Chilled Asparagus Soup

This delicate, pale green soup, garnished with a swirl of cream or yogurt, is as pretty as it is delicious.

INGREDIENTS

Serves 6

900g/2lb fresh asparagus

60ml/4 tbsp butter or olive oil

175g/6oz/1½ cups sliced leeks or
   spring onions (scallions)

45ml/3 tbsp flour

1.5 litres/2½ pints/6¼ cups chicken stock
   or water

120ml/4fl oz/½ cup single (light) cream
   or natural (plain) yogurt

15ml/1 tbsp chopped fresh tarragon
   or chervil

salt and freshly ground black pepper

1 Cut the top 6cm/2½in off the asparagus spears and blanch the tips in boiling water for 5–6 minutes until just tender. Drain thoroughly. Cut each tip into two or three pieces and set aside.

2 Trim the ends of the stalks, removing any brown or woody parts. Chop the stalks into 1cm/½in pieces.

3 Heat the butter or oil in a heavy pan until gently bubbling. Add the sliced leeks or spring onions and cook over a low heat for 5–8 minutes until softened but not browned. Stir in the chopped asparagus stalks, cover and cook for another 6–8 minutes until the stalks are tender.

4 Add the flour and stir well to blend. Cook for 3–4 minutes, uncovered, stirring occasionally.

5 Add the stock or water. Bring to the boil, stirring frequently, then reduce the heat and simmer for 30 minutes. Season with salt and pepper.

6 Purée the soup in a food processor or food mill. If necessary, strain it to remove any coarse fibres. Stir in the asparagus tips, most of the cream or yogurt, and the herbs. Chill well. Stir before serving and check the seasoning. Garnish each bowl with a swirl of cream or yogurt.

Gazpacho

This is a traditional, chilled Spanish soup, perfect for a summer lunch. Make sure that all the ingredients are in peak condition for the best-flavoured soup.

INGREDIENTS

Serves 6

1 green (bell) pepper, seeded
   and chopped
1 red (bell) pepper, seeded and chopped
½ cucumber, roughly chopped
1 onion, roughly chopped
1 fresh red chilli, seeded and
   roughly chopped
450g/1lb ripe plum tomatoes,
   roughly chopped
900ml/1½ pints/3¾ cups passata (bottled
   strained tomatoes) or tomato juice
30ml/2 tbsp red wine vinegar
30ml/2 tbsp olive oil
15ml/1 tbsp caster (superfine) sugar
salt and freshly ground black pepper
crushed ice, to garnish (optional)

1 Reserve a small piece of green and red pepper, cucumber and onion. Finely chop these and set aside as a garnish.

2 Process all the remaining ingredients (except the ice) in a blender or food processor until smooth. You may need to do this in batches.

3 Pass the soup through a sieve into a clean glass bowl, pushing it through with a spoon to extract the maximum amount of flavour.

4 Adjust the seasoning and chill. Serve sprinkled with the reserved chopped green and red pepper, cucumber and onion. For an extra special touch, add a little crushed ice to the garnish.

Vichyssoise

Serve this flavourful soup with a spoon of crème fraîche or sour cream and sprinkle with a few chopped fresh chives – or, for special occasions, garnish with a small spoonful of caviar.

INGREDIENTS

Serves 6–8

450g/1lb/about 3 large potatoes, peeled
   and cubed
1.5 litres/2½ pints/6¼ cups chicken stock
350g/12oz leeks, trimmed
150ml/¼ pint/⅔ cup crème fraîche or
   sour cream
salt and freshly ground black pepper
45ml/3 tbsp chopped fresh chives,
   to garnish

1 Put the cubed potatoes and chicken stock in a large pan or flameproof casserole and bring to the boil. Reduce the heat and simmer for 15–20 minutes.

2 Make a slit along the length of each leek and rinse well under cold running water to wash away any soil. Slice thinly.

VARIATION

To make a low-fat soup, use low-fat fromage frais instead of crème fraîche or sour cream.

3 When the potatoes are barely tender, stir in the leeks. Taste then season with salt and freshly ground black pepper and simmer for 10–15 minutes until both the vegetables are soft, stirring from time to time. If the soup is too thick, thin it down with a little more stock or water.

4 Purée the soup in a blender or food processor. If you prefer a very smooth soup, pass it through a food mill or press through a coarse sieve. Stir in most of the cream, cool and then chill. To serve, ladle into chilled bowls and garnish with a swirl of cream and the chopped chives.

Watercress and Orange Soup

V

This is a healthy and refreshing soup, which is just as good served either hot or chilled.

INGREDIENTS

Serves 4

1 large onion, chopped

15ml/1 tbsp olive oil

2 bunches or bags of watercress

grated rind and juice of 1 large orange

600ml/1 pint/2½ cups vegetable stock

150ml/¼ pint/⅔ cup single (light) cream

10ml/2 tsp cornflour (cornstarch)

salt and freshly ground black pepper

a little thick (heavy) cream or natural
  (plain) yogurt, to garnish

4 orange wedges, to serve

1 Soften the onion in the oil in a large pan. Add the watercress, unchopped, to the onion. Cover and cook for about 5 minutes until the watercress is softened.

2 Add the orange rind and juice and the stock to the watercress mixture. Bring to the boil, cover and simmer for 10–15 minutes.

3 Blend or process the soup thoroughly, and sieve if you want to increase the smoothness of the finished soup. Blend the cream with the cornflour until no lumps remain, then add to the soup. Season to taste.

4 Bring the soup gently back to the boil, stirring until just slightly thickened. Check and adjust the seasoning.

5 Serve the soup with a swirl of cream or yogurt, and a wedge of orange to squeeze in at the last moment.

6 If serving the soup chilled, thicken as above and leave to cool, before chilling in the refrigerator. Garnish with cream or yogurt and orange, as above.

Summer Tomato Soup

The success of this soup depends on having ripe, full-flavoured tomatoes, such as the oval plum variety, so make it when the tomato season is at its peak.

INGREDIENTS

Serves 4

15ml/1 tbsp olive oil

1 large onion, chopped

1 carrot, chopped

1kg/2¼lb ripe tomatoes, quartered

2 garlic cloves, chopped

5 sprigs of fresh thyme, or 1.5ml/¼ tsp dried thyme

4 or 5 sprigs of fresh marjoram, or 1.5ml/¼ tsp dried marjoram

1 bay leaf

45ml/3 tbsp crème fraîche, sour cream or natural (plain) yogurt, plus a little extra to garnish

salt and freshly ground black pepper

1 Heat the olive oil in a large, preferably stainless-steel pan or flameproof casserole.

2 Add the onion and carrot and cook over a medium heat for 3–4 minutes until just softened, stirring occasionally.

3 Add the quartered tomatoes, chopped garlic and herbs. Reduce the heat and simmer, covered, for 30 minutes.

4 Discard the bay leaf and press through a sieve. Leave to cool, then chill in the refrigerator. Serve with a blob of crème fraîche, sour cream or yogurt.

VARIATION

If you prefer, you can use oregano instead of marjoram, and parsley instead of thyme.

Melon and Basil Soup

V

This is a deliciously refreshing, chilled fruit soup, just right for a hot summer's day.

INGREDIENTS

Serves 4–6

2 Charentais or rock melons

75g/3oz/½ cup caster (superfine) sugar

175ml/6fl oz/¾ cup water

finely grated rind and juice of 1 lime

45ml/3 tbsp shredded fresh basil, plus
   whole leaves, to garnish

1 Cut the melons in half across the middle. Scrape out the seeds and discard. Using a melon baller, scoop out 20–24 balls and set aside for the garnish. Scoop out the remaining flesh and place in a blender or food processor.

COOK'S TIP

~

Add the syrup in two stages, as the amount of sugar needed will depend on the sweetness of the melon.

2 Place the sugar, water and lime rind in a small pan over a low heat. Stir until dissolved, bring to the boil and simmer for 2–3 minutes. Remove from the heat and leave to cool slightly. Pour half the mixture into the blender or food processor with the melon flesh. Blend until smooth, adding the remaining syrup and lime juice to taste.

3 Pour the mixture into a bowl, stir in the shredded basil and chill. Serve garnished with whole basil leaves and the reserved melon balls.

Tomato and Fresh Basil Soup

This is the perfect soup for late summer when fresh tomatoes are at their most flavoursome.

INGREDIENTS

Serves 4–6

15ml/1 tbsp olive oil
25g/1oz/2 tbsp butter
1 medium onion, finely chopped
900g/2lb Italian plum tomatoes, chopped
1 garlic clove, roughly chopped
about 750ml/1¼ pints/3 cups chicken
   or vegetable stock
120ml/4 fl oz/½ cup dry white wine
30ml/2 tbsp sun-dried tomato
   purée (paste)
30ml/2 tbsp shredded fresh basil, plus
   a few whole leaves to garnish
150ml/¼ pint/⅔ cup double (heavy) cream
salt and freshly ground black pepper

1 Heat the oil and butter in a large pan until foaming. Add the onion and cook gently for about 5 minutes, stirring frequently, until softened, but do not allow to brown.

2 Stir in the chopped tomatoes and garlic, then add the stock, white wine and sun-dried tomato purée, with salt and pepper to taste. Bring to the boil, then lower the heat, half-cover the pan and simmer gently for 20 minutes, stirring occasionally to stop the tomatoes sticking to the base.

3 Process the soup with the shredded basil in a food processor or blender, then press through a sieve into a clean pan.

4 Add the cream and heat through, stirring constantly. Do not allow the soup to approach boiling point. Check the consistency and add more stock, if necessary. Adjust the seasoning to taste, pour into heated bowls and garnish with whole basil leaves. Serve immediately.

Cucumber and Yogurt Soup with Walnuts

V

This is a particularly refreshing cold soup, using a classic combination of cucumber and yogurt.

INGREDIENTS

Serves 5–6

1 cucumber

4 garlic cloves, peeled

2.5ml/½ tsp salt

75g/3oz/¾ cup walnut pieces

40g/1½oz day-old bread, torn into pieces

30ml/2 tbsp walnut or sunflower oil

400ml/14fl oz/1⅔ cups natural (plain) yogurt

120ml/4fl oz/½ cup cold water or chilled still mineral water

5–10ml/1–2 tsp lemon juice

For the garnish

40g/1½oz/½ cup walnuts, chopped

25ml/1½ tbsp olive oil

sprigs of fresh dill

1 Cut the cucumber in half and peel one half of it. Dice the cucumber flesh and set aside.

2 Using a large mortar and pestle, crush together the garlic and salt well, then add the walnuts and bread.

3 When the mixture is smooth, slowly add the walnut or sunflower oil and combine well.

COOK'S TIP

If you prefer your soup smooth, purée it in a food processor or blender before serving.

4 Transfer the mixture into a large bowl and beat in the yogurt and diced cucumber. Add the cold water or mineral water and lemon juice to taste.

5 Pour the soup into chilled soup bowls to serve. Garnish with the chopped walnuts and drizzle with the olive oil. Finally, arrange the sprigs of dill on top and serve immediately.

Chilled Almond Soup

Unless you are prepared to spend time pounding all the ingredients for this soup by hand, a food processor is essential. Then you'll find that this Spanish soup is simple to make and refreshing to eat on a hot day.

INGREDIENTS

Serves 6

115g/4oz fresh white bread
750ml/1¼ pints/3 cups cold water
115g/4oz/1 cup blanched almonds
2 garlic cloves, sliced
75ml/5 tbsp olive oil
25ml/1½ tbsp sherry vinegar
salt and freshly ground black pepper

For the garnish
toasted flaked (sliced) almonds
seedless green and black grapes, halved
    and with skins removed

1 Break the bread into a bowl and pour 150ml/¼ pint/ ⅔ cup of the water on top. Leave for 5 minutes.

2 Put the almonds and garlic in a blender or food processor and process until finely ground. Blend in the soaked bread.

3 Gradually add the oil until the mixture forms a smooth paste. Add the sherry vinegar, then the remaining cold water and process until smooth.

4 Transfer to a bowl and season with salt and pepper, adding a little more water if the soup is too thick. Chill for at least 2–3 hours. Serve scattered with the toasted almonds and grapes.

Beetroot and Apricot Swirl

This soup is most attractive if you swirl together the two differently coloured mixtures, but if you prefer they can be mixed together to save on both time and washing up.

INGREDIENTS

Serves 4

4 large cooked beetroots (beets),
  roughly chopped
1 small onion, roughly chopped
600ml/1 pint/2½ cups chicken stock
200g/7oz/1 cup ready-to-eat
  dried apricots
250ml/8fl oz/1 cup orange juice
salt and freshly ground black pepper

2 Place the rest of the onion in a pan with the apricots and orange juice, cover and simmer gently for about 15 minutes, until tender. Purée in a food processor or blender.

3 Return the two mixtures to the pans and reheat. Season to taste with salt and pepper, then swirl them together in individual soup bowls for a marbled effect.

1 Place the roughly chopped beetroot and half the onion in a pan with the stock. Bring to the boil, then reduce the heat, cover and simmer for about 10 minutes. Place the mixture in a food processor or blender and purée until smooth.

COOK'S TIP

The apricot mixture should be the same consistency as the beetroot (beet) mixture – if it is too thick, add a little more orange juice.

Green Pea and Mint Soup

Perfect partners, peas and mint really capture the flavours of summer.

INGREDIENTS

Serves 4

50g/2oz/4 tbsp butter
4 spring onions (scallions), chopped
450g/1lb fresh or frozen peas
600ml/1 pint/2½ cups vegetable stock
2 large sprigs of fresh mint
600ml/1 pint/2½ cups milk
a pinch of sugar (optional)
salt and freshly ground black pepper
small sprigs of fresh mint, to garnish
single (light) cream, to serve

1 Heat the butter in a large pan, add the chopped spring onions and cook gently on a low heat until they are softened but not browned.

2 Stir the peas into the pan, add the stock and mint, and bring to the boil. Cover and simmer gently for about 30 minutes if you are using fresh peas (15 minutes if you are using frozen peas), until they are tender. Remove about 45ml/3 tbsp of the peas, and reserve to use for a garnish.

3 Pour the soup into a food processor or blender, add the milk and purée until smooth. Season to taste, adding a pinch of sugar, if liked. Leave to cool, then chill lightly in the refrigerator.

4 Pour the soup into bowls. Swirl a little cream into each, then garnish with the mint and the reserved peas.

Carrot Soup with Ginger

The zing of fresh ginger is an ideal complement to the sweetness of cooked carrots.

INGREDIENTS

Serves 6

25g/1oz/2 tbsp butter or margarine

1 onion, chopped

1 celery stick, chopped

1 medium potato, chopped

675g/1½lb carrots, chopped

10ml/2 tsp minced (ground) fresh
   root ginger

1.2 litres/2 pints/5 cups chicken stock

105ml/7 tbsp whipping cream

a good pinch of freshly grated nutmeg

salt and freshly ground black pepper

1 Combine the butter or margarine, onion and celery and cook for about 5 minutes until softened.

2 Stir in the potato, carrots, ginger and stock. Bring to the boil. Reduce the heat to low, cover and simmer for about 20 minutes.

3 Pour the soup into a food processor or blender and process until it is smooth. Alternatively, use a vegetable mill to purée the soup. Return the soup to the pan. Stir in the cream and nutmeg and add salt and pepper to taste. Reheat gently to serve.

Carrot and Coriander Soup

Use a good home-made stock for this soup for a real depth of flavour.

INGREDIENTS

Serves 4

50g/2oz/4 tbsp butter

3 leeks, sliced

450g/1lb carrots, sliced

15ml/1 tbsp ground coriander

1.2 litres/2 pints/5 cups chicken stock

150ml/¼ pint/⅔ cup Greek
  (US strained plain) yogurt

salt and freshly ground black pepper

30–45ml/2–3 tbsp chopped fresh
  coriander (cilantro), to garnish

3 Leave to cool slightly, then purée the soup in a blender until smooth. Return the soup to the pan and add 30ml/2 tbsp of the yogurt, then taste the soup and adjust the seasoning. Reheat gently, but do not boil.

4 Ladle the soup into bowls and put a spoonful of the remaining yogurt in the centre of each. Sprinkle over the chopped coriander and serve immediately.

1 Melt the butter in a large pan. Add the leeks and carrots and stir well. Cover and cook for 10 minutes, until the vegetables are beginning to soften.

2 Stir in the ground coriander and cook for about 1 minute. Pour in the stock and add seasoning to taste. Bring to the boil, cover and simmer for about 20 minutes, until the leeks and carrots are tender.

Mushroom, Celery and Garlic Soup

A robust soup in which the dominant flavour of mushrooms is enhanced with garlic, while celery introduces a contrasting note.

INGREDIENTS

Serves 4

350g/12oz/4½ cups chopped mushrooms

4 celery sticks, chopped

3 garlic cloves

45ml/3 tbsp dry sherry or white wine

750ml/1¼ pints/3 cups chicken stock

30ml/2 tbsp Worcestershire sauce

5ml/1 tsp freshly grated nutmeg

salt and freshly ground black pepper

celery leaves, to garnish

1 Place the mushrooms, celery and garlic in a pan and stir in the sherry or wine. Cover and cook over a low heat for 30–40 minutes until the vegetables are tender.

2 Add half the stock and purée in a food processor or blender until smooth. Return to the pan and add the remaining stock, the Worcestershire sauce and nutmeg.

3 Bring to the boil and season to taste with salt and pepper. Serve hot, garnished with celery leaves.

Chicken Stellette Soup

Simple and quick to prepare, provided you have some good stock to hand, this light, clear soup is easy on the palate.

INGREDIENTS

Serves 4–6

900ml/1½ pints/3¾ cups chicken stock

1 bay leaf

4 spring onions (scallions), sliced

225g/8oz button (white)
   mushrooms, sliced

115g/4oz cooked chicken breast

50g/2oz small soup pasta (stellette)

150ml/¼ pint/⅔ cup dry white wine

15ml/1 tbsp chopped parsley

salt and freshly ground black pepper

1 Put the stock and bay leaf into a large pan and bring to the boil. Add the sliced spring onions and mushrooms.

2 Remove the skin from the chicken and discard. Slice the chicken thinly, add to the soup and season to taste with salt and pepper. Heat through for 2–3 minutes.

3 Add the pasta to the soup, cover and simmer for 7–8 minutes until the pasta is *al dente*.

4 Just before serving, add the wine and chopped parsley and heat through for 2–3 minutes. Pour in to individual soup bowls.

Courgette Soup with Pasta

This is a pretty, fresh-tasting soup, which is always a welcome dish in hot weather.

INGREDIENTS

Serves 4–6

60ml/4 tbsp olive or sunflower oil

2 onions, finely chopped

1.5 litres/2½ pints/6¼ cups chicken stock

900g/21b courgettes (zucchini)

115g/4oz small soup pasta (stellette)

a little lemon juice

30ml/2 tbsp chopped fresh chervil

salt and freshly ground black pepper

sour cream, to serve

1 Heat the oil in a large pan and add the onions. Cover and cook gently for about 20 minutes, stirring occasionally, until soft but not coloured.

2 Add the stock to the pan and bring the mixture to the boil.

3 Meanwhile, grate the courgettes and stir into the boiling stock with the pasta. Reduce the heat, cover the pan and simmer for 15 minutes until the pasta is tender.

4 Season to taste with lemon juice, salt and pepper. Stir in the chopped fresh chervil. Pour into bowls and add a swirl of sour cream before serving.

VARIATION

You can use cucumber instead of courgettes (zucchini), if you prefer, and other soup pasta such as tiny shells.

Spinach and Beancurd Soup

This is an extremely delicate and mild-flavoured soup, which can be used to counterbalance the heat from a hot Thai curry.

INGREDIENTS

Serves 4–6

30ml/2 tbsp dried shrimps

1 litre/1¾ pints/4 cups chicken stock

225g/8oz fresh beancurd (tofu), drained
  and cut into 2cm/¾in cubes

30ml/2 tbsp fish sauce (nam pla)

350g/12oz fresh spinach

freshly ground black pepper

2 spring onions (scallions), finely sliced,
  to garnish

1 Rinse and drain the dried shrimps. Combine the shrimps with the chicken stock in a large pan and bring to the boil. Add the beancurd and simmer for about 5 minutes. Season with fish sauce and black pepper to taste.

2 Wash the spinach leaves thoroughly and tear into bitesize pieces. Add to the soup. Cook for another 1–2 minutes.

3 Pour the soup into warmed bowls, sprinkle the chopped spring onions on top to garnish, and serve.

Chinese Beancurd and Lettuce Soup

*This light, clear soup is brimful
of colourful, tasty vegetables.*

INGREDIENTS

Serves 4

30ml/2 tbsp groundnut (peanut) oil

200g/7oz smoked or marinated beancurd
(tofu) cubed

3 spring onions (scallions), sliced

2 garlic cloves, cut into thin strips

1 carrot, finely sliced into rounds

1 litre/1¾ pints/4 cups vegetable stock

30ml/2 tbsp soy sauce

15ml/l tbsp dry sherry or vermouth

5ml/1 tsp sugar

115g/4oz cos (romaine) lettuce, shredded

salt and freshly ground black pepper

1 Heat the oil in a preheated
wok, then add the beancurd
cubes and stir-fry until browned.
Drain on kitchen paper and
set aside.

2 Add the spring onions, garlic
and carrot to the wok and stir-
fry for 2 minutes. Add the stock,
soy sauce, sherry or vermouth,
sugar, lettuce and fried beancurd.
Heat through gently for 1 minute,
season to taste and serve.

Chinese Chicken and Asparagus Soup

This is a very delicate and delicious soup. When fresh asparagus is not in season, canned white asparagus is an acceptable substitute.

INGREDIENTS

Serves 4

140g/5oz chicken breast fillet
pinch of salt
1 tsp egg white
1 tsp cornflour (cornstarch) paste
115g/4oz asparagus
700ml/1¼ pints/3 cups chicken stock
salt and freshly ground black pepper
fresh coriander (cilantro) leaves,
    to garnish

1 Cut the chicken meat into thin slices each about the size of a postage stamp. Mix with a pinch of salt, then add the egg white, and finally the cornflour paste.

2 Cut off and discard the tough stems of the asparagus, and diagonally cut the tender spears into short, even lengths.

3 In a wok or pan, bring the stock to a rolling boil, add the asparagus and bring back to the boil, cooking for 2 minutes. (You do not need to do this if you are using canned asparagus.)

4 Add the chicken, stir to separate and bring back to the boil once more. Adjust the seasonings. Serve hot, garnished with fresh coriander leaves.

Duck Consommé

The Vietnamese community in France has had a profound influence on French cooking, as this soup bears witness – it is light and rich at the same time, with intriguing flavours of south-east Asia.

INGREDIENTS

Serves 4

1 duck carcass (raw or cooked), plus 2 legs or any giblets, trimmed of as much fat as possible

1 large onion, unpeeled, with root end trimmed

2 carrots, cut into 5cm/2in pieces

1 parsnip, cut into 5cm/2in pieces

1 leek, cut into 5cm/2in pieces

2–4 garlic cloves, crushed

2.5cm/1in piece fresh root ginger, peeled and sliced

15ml/1 tbsp black peppercorns

4–6 sprigs of fresh thyme or 5ml/1 tsp dried thyme

1 small bunch of coriander (cilantro) (6–8 sprigs), leaves and stems separated

For the garnish

1 small carrot

1 small leek, halved lengthways

4–6 shiitake mushrooms, thinly sliced

soy sauce

2 spring onions (scallions), thinly sliced

watercress or finely shredded Chinese leaves (Chinese cabbage)

freshly ground black pepper

1 Put the duck carcass and legs or giblets, onion, carrots, parsnip, leek and garlic in a large, heavy pan or flameproof casserole. Add the ginger, peppercorns, thyme and coriander stems, cover with cold water and bring to the boil over a medium-high heat, skimming off any foam that rises to the surface.

2 Reduce the heat and simmer for 1½–2 hours, then strain through a muslin- (cheesecloth-) lined sieve into a bowl, discarding the bones and vegetables. Cool the stock and chill for several hours or overnight. Skim off any congealed fat and blot the surface with kitchen paper.

3 To make the garnish, cut the carrot and leek into 5cm/2in pieces. Cut each piece lengthways in thin slices, then stack and slice into thin julienne strips. Place in a large pan with the sliced mushrooms.

4 Pour over the stock and add a few dashes of soy sauce and some pepper. Bring to the boil over a medium-high heat, skimming any foam that rises to the surface. Adjust the seasoning. Stir in the spring onions and watercress or Chinese leaves. Ladle the consommé into warmed bowls and sprinkle with the coriander leaves before serving.

  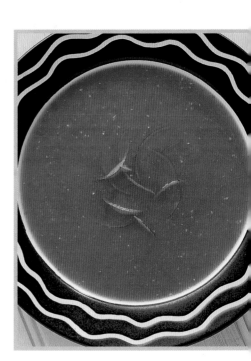

HOT &
SPICY SOUPS

Jalapeño-style Soup

Chicken, chilli and avocado combine to make this simple but unusual soup.

INGREDIENTS

Serves 6

1.5 litres/2½ pints/6¼ cups chicken stock

2 cooked chicken breast fillets, skinned
   and cut into large strips

1 drained canned chipotle or jalapeño
   chilli, rinsed

1 avocado

COOK'S TIP

~

When using canned chillies,
it is important to rinse them
thoroughly before adding them
to a dish so as to remove the
flavour of any pickling liquid.

1 Heat the stock in a large pan and add the chicken and chilli. Simmer over a very gentle heat for 5 minutes to heat the chicken through and release the flavour from the chilli.

2 Cut the avocado in half, remove the stone (pit) and peel off the skin. Slice the avocado flesh neatly lengthways.

3 Using a slotted spoon, remove the chilli from the stock and discard it. Pour the soup into heated serving bowls, distributing the chicken evenly among them.

4 Carefully add a few avocado slices to each bowl and serve the soup immediately.

Miami Chilled Avocado Soup

Avocados are combined with lemon juice, dry sherry and an optional dash of hot pepper sauce, to make this subtle chilled soup.

INGREDIENTS

Serves 4

2 large or 3 medium ripe avocados

15ml/1 tbsp fresh lemon juice

75g/3oz/³⁄₄ cup coarsely chopped
    peeled cucumber

30ml/2 tbsp dry sherry

25g/1oz/¼ cup coarsely chopped spring
    onions (scallions)

475ml/16fl oz/2 cups mild-flavoured
    chicken stock

5ml/1 tsp salt

hot pepper sauce (optional)

natural (plain) yogurt, to garnish

1 Cut the avocados in half, remove the stones (pits) and peel. Roughly chop the flesh and place in a food processor or blender. Add the lemon juice and process until very smooth.

2 Add the cucumber, sherry and most of the spring onions, reserving a few for the garnish. Process again until smooth.

3 In a large bowl, combine the avocado mixture with the chicken stock. Whisk until well blended. Season with the salt and a few drops of hot pepper sauce, if liked. Cover the bowl and place in the refrigerator to chill thoroughly.

4 To serve, fill individual bowls with the soup. Place a spoonful of yogurt in the centre of each bowl and swirl with a spoon. Sprinkle with the reserved chopped spring onions.

Curried Celery Soup

V

An unusual but stimulating combination of flavours, this warming soup is an excellent way to transform celery. Serve with warm bread rolls.

INGREDIENTS

Serves 4–6

10ml/2 tsp olive oil

1 onion, chopped

1 leek, sliced

675g/1½lb celery, chopped

15ml/1 tbsp medium or hot curry powder

225g/8oz unpeeled potatoes, washed and diced

900ml/1½ pints/3¾ cups vegetable stock

bouquet garni

30ml/2 tbsp chopped fresh mixed herbs

salt

celery seeds and leaves, to garnish

COOK'S TIP

For a change, use celeriac and sweet potatoes in place of celery and standard potatoes.

1 Heat the oil in a large pan. Add the onion, leek and celery, cover and cook gently for about 10 minutes, stirring occasionally.

2 Add the curry powder and cook gently for 2 minutes, stirring from time to time.

3 Add the potatoes, stock and bouquet garni, cover and bring to the boil. Simmer for about 20 minutes, until the vegetables are tender, but not too soft.

4 Remove and discard the bouquet garni and set the soup aside to cool slightly before processing.

5 Transfer the soup to a blender or food processor and process in batches until smooth.

6 Add the mixed herbs, season to taste and process briefly again. Return to the pan and reheat gently until piping hot. Ladle into bowls and garnish each one with a sprinkling of celery seeds and a few celery leaves before serving.

Spinach and Rice Soup

Use very fresh, young spinach leaves and risotto rice to prepare this surprisingly light, refreshing soup.

INGREDIENTS

Serves 4

675g/1½lb fresh spinach, washed
45ml/3 tbsp extra-virgin olive oil
1 small onion, finely chopped
2 garlic cloves, finely chopped
1 small fresh red chilli, seeded and
    finely chopped
115g/4oz/generous ½ cup risotto rice
1.2 litres/2 pints/5 cups vegetable stock
salt and freshly ground black pepper
60ml/4 tbsp grated Pecorino cheese,
    to serve

1 Place the spinach in a large pan with just the water that clings to its leaves after washing. Add a large pinch of salt. Heat gently until the spinach has wilted, then remove from the heat and drain, reserving any liquid. Use a knife to chop finely.

2 Heat the oil in a large pan and cook the onion, garlic and chilli for 4–5 minutes until softened. Stir in the rice until well coated, then pour in the stock and reserved spinach liquid.

3 Bring to the boil, lower the heat and simmer gently for 10 minutes. Add the spinach and cook for 5–7 minutes more, until the rice is tender. Season with salt and freshly ground pepper and serve with the Pecorino cheese.

Spicy Carrot Soup with Garlic Croûtons

V

Carrot soup is given a touch of spice with coriander, cumin and chilli powder.

INGREDIENTS

Serves 6

15ml/l tbsp olive oil

1 large onion, chopped

675g/1½lb/3¾ cups carrots, sliced

5ml/1 tsp each ground coriander, ground cumin and hot chilli powder

900ml/1½ pints/3¾ cups vegetable stock

salt and freshly ground black pepper

sprigs of fresh coriander (cilantro), to garnish

For the garlic croûtons

a little olive oil

2 garlic cloves, crushed

4 slices bread, crusts removed, cut into 1cm/½in cubes

1 To make the soup, heat the oil in a large pan, add the onion and carrots and cook gently for 5 minutes, stirring occasionally. Add the ground spices and cook gently for 1 minute, continuing to stir.

2 Stir in the stock, bring to the boil, then cover and cook gently for about 45 minutes until the carrots are tender.

3 Meanwhile, make the garlic croûtons. Heat the oil in a frying pan, add the garlic and cook gently for 30 seconds, stirring. Add the bread cubes, turn them over in the oil and fry over a medium heat for a few minutes until crisp and golden brown all over, turning frequently. Drain on kitchen paper and keep warm.

4 Purée the soup in a blender or food processor until smooth, then season to taste with salt and pepper. Return the soup to the rinsed-out pan and reheat gently. Serve hot, sprinkled with garlic croûtons and garnished with coriander sprigs.

Curried Carrot and Apple Soup

The combination of carrot, curry and apple is a highly successful one. Curried fruit is delicious.

Serves 4

10ml/2 tsp sunflower oil
15ml/1 tbsp mild Korma curry powder
500g/1¼lb carrots, chopped
1 large onion, chopped
1 tart cooking apple, chopped
750ml/1¼ pints/3 cups chicken stock
salt and freshly ground black pepper
natural (plain) yogurt and carrot curls,
    to garnish

1 Heat the oil in a large, heavy pan and gently fry the curry powder for 2–3 minutes.

2 Add the chopped carrots and onion and the cooking apple, stir well until coated with the curry powder, then cover the pan.

3 Cook over a low heat for about 15 minutes, shaking the pan occasionally, until softened. Spoon the vegetable mixture into a food processor or blender, then add half the stock and process until smooth.

4 Return to the pan and pour in the remaining stock. Bring the soup to the boil and adjust the seasoning before serving in bowls, garnished with a swirl of yogurt and a few curls of raw carrot.

Leek, Parsnip and Ginger Soup

V

A flavoursome winter warmer, with the added spiciness of fresh ginger.

INGREDIENTS

Serves 4–6

30ml/2 tbsp olive oil

225g/8oz/2 cups leeks, sliced

25g/1oz fresh root ginger, peeled and finely chopped

675g/1½lb/5 cups parsnips, roughly chopped

300ml/½ pint/l¼ cups dry white wine

1.2 litres/2 pints/5 cups vegetable stock or water

salt and freshly ground black pepper

fromage blanc, to garnish

paprika, to garnish

1 Heat the oil in a large pan and add the leeks and ginger. Cook gently for 2–3 minutes until the leeks start to soften.

2 Add the parsnips and cook for a further 7–8 minutes until they are beginning to soften.

3 Pour in the wine and stock or water and bring to the boil. Reduce the heat and simmer for 20–30 minutes or until the parsnips are tender.

4 Purée in a blender or food processor until smooth. Season to taste. Reheat and garnish with a swirl of fromage blanc and a light dusting of paprika.

Spicy Tomato and Coriander Soup

Although soups are not often eaten in India or Pakistan, tomato soup seems to be favoured. Deliciously spicy, it is also the perfect soup to prepare for a cold winter's day.

INGREDIENTS

Serves 4

675g/1¹/₂lb tomatoes

30ml/2 tbsp vegetable oil

1 bay leaf

4 spring onions (scallions), chopped

5ml/1 tsp salt

2.5ml/¹/₂ tsp crushed garlic

5ml/1 tsp crushed black peppercorns

30ml/2 tbsp chopped fresh coriander (cilantro)

750ml/1¹/₄ pints/3 cups water

15ml/1 tbsp cornflour (cornstarch)

For the garnish

1 spring onion (scallion), chopped

30ml/2 tbsp single (light) cream

COOK'S TIP

If the only fresh tomatoes available are rather pale and under-ripe, add 15ml/1 tbsp tomato purée (paste) to the pan with the chopped tomatoes. This will enhance the colour and flavour of the soup.

1 To peel the tomatoes, plunge them into very hot water, then lift them out more or less straight away using a slotted spoon. The skin should now peel off quickly and easily. Once this is done, chop the tomatoes roughly.

2 In a medium-size pan, heat the oil and cook the chopped tomatoes, bay leaf and chopped spring onions for a few minutes until soft and translucent, but not browned.

3 Gradually add the salt, garlic, peppercorns and fresh coriander to the tomato mixture, finally adding the water.

4 Bring to the boil, lower the heat and simmer gently for 15–20 minutes. Meanwhile, dissolve the cornflour in a little cold water, and set aside.

5 Remove the soup from the heat and press the contents of the pan through a sieve placed over a bowl.

6 Return the soup to the pan, add the cornflour mixture and stir over a gentle heat for about 3 minutes until thickened.

7 Pour into individual soup bowls and garnish with the chopped spring onion and a swirl of cream. Serve piping hot.

South Indian Pepper Water

V

This is a highly stimulating broth for cold winter evenings. Serve with the whole spices or strain and reheat as desired. The lemon juice may be adjusted to taste, but this dish should be distinctly sour.

INGREDIENTS

Serves 2–4

30ml/2 tbsp vegetable oil

2.5ml/½ tsp freshly ground black pepper

5ml/1 tsp cumin seeds

2.5ml/½ tsp mustard seeds

1.5ml/¼ tsp asafoetida powder

2 whole dried red chillies

4–6 curry leaves

2.5ml/½ tsp ground turmeric

2 garlic cloves, crushed

300ml/½ pint/1¼ cups tomato juice

juice of 2 lemons

120ml/4fl oz/½ cup water

salt

fresh coriander (cilantro) leaves, chopped, to garnish

1 In a large frying pan, heat the vegetable oil and cook the spices and garlic until the chillies are nearly black and the garlic is a golden brown.

2 Lower the heat and add the tomato juice, lemon juice, water and salt to taste. Bring to the boil, then simmer for 10 minutes. Garnish with chopped coriander and serve piping hot.

COOK'S TIP

Asafoetida is a pungent powder used to enhance Indian vegetarian cooking. In its raw state it can smell quite unpleasant but this smell soon disappears once it is added to your cooking.

Red Pepper Soup with Lime

The beautiful, rich red colour of this soup makes it an attractive light lunch. For a special occasion, toast some tiny croûtons and serve these sprinkled into the soup.

INGREDIENTS

Serves 4–6

1 large onion, chopped

4 red (bell) peppers, seeded and chopped

5ml/1 tsp olive oil

1 garlic clove, crushed

1 small fresh red chilli, sliced

45ml/3 tbsp tomato purée (paste)

900ml/1½ pints/3¾ cups chicken stock

finely grated rind and juice of 1 lime

salt and freshly ground black pepper

shreds of lime rind, to garnish

1 Cook the onion and peppers gently in the oil in a covered pan for about 5 minutes, shaking the pan occasionally, until they are just softened.

2 Stir in the garlic, chilli and tomato purée. Add half the stock, then bring to the boil. Cover and simmer for 10 minutes.

3 Cool slightly, then purée in a food processor or blender. Return to the pan and add the remaining stock, the lime rind and juice and salt and pepper.

4 Bring the soup back to the boil, then serve at once, with a few strips of lime rind scattered into each bowl.

V

Spicy Peanut Soup

A thick and warming vegetable soup, flavoured with hot and spicy chilli and peanuts.

INGREDIENTS

Serves 6

30ml/2 tbsp oil

1 large onion, finely chopped

2 garlic cloves, crushed

5ml/1 tsp mild chilli powder

2 red (bell) peppers, seeded and chopped

225g/8oz carrots, finely chopped

225g/8oz potatoes, finely chopped

3 celery sticks, sliced

900ml/1½ pints/3¾ cups vegetable stock

90ml/6 tbsp crunchy peanut butter

115g/4oz/⅔ cup sweetcorn

salt and freshly ground black pepper

roughly chopped unsalted roasted
    peanuts, to garnish

1 Heat the oil in a large pan and cook the onion and garlic for about 3 minutes. Add the chilli powder and cook for a further 1 minute.

2 Add the red peppers, carrots, potatoes and celery. Stir well, then cook for a further 4 minutes, stirring occasionally.

3 Add the vegetable stock, followed by the peanut butter and sweetcorn. Stir until thoroughly combined.

4 Season well. Bring to the boil, cover and simmer for about 20 minutes until all the vegetables are tender. Adjust the seasoning before serving, sprinkled with the chopped peanuts.

Spiced Lentil Soup

V

A subtle blend of spices takes this warming soup to new heights. Serve it with crusty bread for a filling and satisfying lunch.

INGREDIENTS

Serves 6

2 onions, finely chopped

2 garlic cloves, crushed

4 tomatoes, roughly chopped

2.5ml/½ tsp ground turmeric

5ml/1 tsp ground cumin

6 cardamom pods

½ cinnamon stick

225g/8oz/1 cup red lentils, rinsed
  and drained

900ml/1½ pints/3¾ cups water

400g/14oz can coconut milk

15ml/1 tbsp lime juice

salt and freshly ground black pepper

cumin seeds, to garnish

1 Put the onions, garlic, tomatoes, turmeric, cumin, cardamom pods, cinnamon, lentils and water into a pan. Bring to the boil, lower the heat, cover and simmer gently for 20 minutes or until the lentils are soft.

2 Remove the cardamom pods and cinnamon stick, then purée the mixture in a blender or food processor. Press the soup through a sieve, then return it to the clean pan.

3 Reserve a little of the coconut milk for the garnish and add the remainder to the pan with the lime juice. Stir well and season with salt and pepper. Reheat the soup gently without boiling. Swirl in the reserved coconut milk, garnish with cumin seeds and serve piping hot.

Hot-and-sour Soup

V

A classic Chinese soup, this is a warming and flavoursome start to a meal.

INGREDIENTS

Serves 4

10g/¼oz dried cloud ears (wood ears)

8 fresh shiitake mushrooms

75g/3oz beancurd (tofu)

50g/2oz/½ cup sliced, drained, canned
    bamboo shoots

900ml/1½ pints/3¾ cups vegetable stock

15ml/1 tbsp caster (superfine) sugar

45ml/3 tbsp rice vinegar

15ml/1 tbsp light soy sauce

1.5ml/¼ tsp chilli oil

2.5ml/½ tsp salt

a large pinch of freshly ground white
    pepper

15ml/1 tbsp cornflour (cornstarch)

15ml/l tbsp cold water

1 egg white

5ml/1 tsp sesame oil

2 spring onions (scallions), cut into fine
    rings, to garnish

COOK'S TIP

To transform this tasty soup into
a nutritious light meal, simply
add extra mushrooms, beancurd
(tofu) and bamboo shoots.

1 Soak the cloud ears in hot water for 30 minutes or until soft. Drain, trim off and discard the hard base from each, and chop the cloud ears roughly.

2 Remove and discard the stalks from the shiitake mushrooms. Cut the caps into thin strips. Cut the beancurd into 1cm/½in cubes and shred the bamboo shoots.

3 Place the stock, mushrooms, beancurd, bamboo shoots and cloud ears in a large pan. Bring the stock to the boil, lower the heat and simmer for about 5 minutes.

4 Stir in the sugar, vinegar, soy sauce, chilli oil, salt and pepper. Mix the cornflour to a paste with the water. Add the mixture to the soup, stirring until it thickens slightly.

5 Lightly beat the egg white, then pour it slowly into the soup in a steady stream, stirring constantly. Cook, stirring, until the egg white changes colour.

6 Add the sesame oil just before serving. Ladle into heated bowls and garnish each portion with spring onion rings.

Hot and Sour Prawn Soup with Lemon Grass

This classic seafood soup, known as Tom Yam Goong, is probably the most popular and best-known soup from Thailand.

INGREDIENTS

Serves 4–6

450g/1lb king prawns (jumbo shrimp)
1 litre/1¾ pints/4 cups chicken stock
3 lemon grass stalks
10 kaffir lime leaves, torn in half
225g/8oz can straw mushrooms, drained
45ml/3 tbsp fish sauce (nam pla)
50ml/2fl oz/¼ cup lime juice
30ml/2 tbsp chopped spring
    onion (scallion)
15ml/1 tbsp fresh coriander
    (cilantro) leaves
4 fresh red chillies, seeded and chopped
2 spring onions (scallions), finely
    chopped, to garnish

1 Shell and devein the prawns. Rinse the prawn shells and place in a large pan with the stock and bring to the boil.

2 Bruise the lemon grass stalks with the blunt edge of a chopping knife and add them to the stock, together with half the lime leaves. Simmer gently for 5–6 minutes until the stalks change colour and the stock is fragrant.

3 Strain the stock through a sieve over a bowl, return the stock to the pan and reheat. Discard the lemon grass stalks. Add the mushrooms and prawns to the liquid, then cook until the prawns turn pink.

4 Stir in the fish sauce, lime juice, spring onion, coriander, red chillies and the rest of the lime leaves. Taste and adjust the seasoning. The soup should be sour, salty, spicy and hot. Garnish with finely chopped spring onions before serving.

Tamarind Soup with Peanuts and Vegetables

Known in Indonesia as Sayur Asam, *this is a colourful and refreshing soup from Jakarta.*

INGREDIENTS

Serves 4 as an appetizer or 8 as part of a buffet

5 shallots or 1 medium red onion, sliced

3 garlic cloves, crushed

2.5cm/1in galangal, peeled and sliced

1–2 fresh red chillies, seeded and sliced

25g/1oz/¼ cup raw peanuts

1cm/½in cube shrimp paste, prepared

1.2 litres/2 pints/5 cups well-flavoured stock

50–75g/2–3oz/½–¾ cup salted peanuts, lightly crushed

15–30ml/1–2 tbsp dark brown sugar

5ml/1 tsp tamarind pulp, soaked in 75ml/5 tbsp warm water for 15 minutes

salt

For the vegetables

1 chayote, thinly peeled, seeds removed, flesh finely sliced

115g/4oz green beans, trimmed and finely sliced

50g/2oz sweetcorn kernels (optional)

a handful of green leaves, such as watercress, rocket (arugula) or Chinese leaves (Chinese cabbage), finely shredded

1 fresh green chilli, sliced, to garnish

1 Grind the shallots or onion, garlic, galangal, chillies, raw peanuts and shrimp paste to a paste in a food processor, or using a mortar and pestle.

2 Pour in some of the stock to moisten and then pour this mixture into a pan or wok, adding the rest of the stock. Cook for 15 minutes with the crushed salted peanuts and sugar.

3 Strain the tamarind pulp, discarding the seeds, and reserve the juice.

4 About 5 minutes before serving, add the chayote slices, beans and sweetcorn, if using, to the soup and cook fairly rapidly. At the last minute, add the green leaves and salt to taste.

5 Add the tamarind juice and adjust the seasoning. Serve immediately, garnished with slices of green chilli.

Fish and Shellfish Soup with Rouille

This is a really chunky, aromatic mixed fish soup from France. Rouille, a fiery hot paste, is served separately for everyone to swirl into their soup to flavour.

Serves 6

3 gurnard or red mullet, scaled and gutted
12 large prawns (shrimp)
675g/1½lb white fish, such as cod, haddock, halibut or monkfish
225g/8oz mussels
1 onion, quartered
1.2 litres/2 pints/5 cups water
5ml/1 tsp saffron threads
75ml/5 tbsp olive oil
1 fennel bulb, roughly chopped
4 garlic cloves, crushed
3 strips pared orange rind
4 sprigs of thyme
675g/1½lb tomatoes or 400g/14oz can chopped tomatoes
30ml/2 tbsp sun-dried tomato purée (paste)
3 bay leaves
salt and freshly ground black pepper

For the rouille

1 red (bell) pepper, seeded and roughly chopped
1 fresh red chilli, seeded and sliced
2 garlic cloves, chopped
75ml/5 tbsp olive oil
15g/½oz/¼ cup fresh breadcrumbs

1 To make the *rouille*, process all the ingredients in a blender or food processor until smooth. Transfer to a serving dish and chill.

COOK'S TIP

To save time, order the fish and ask the fishmonger to fillet the gurnard or mullet for you.

2 Fillet the gurnard or mullet by cutting away the flesh from the backbone. Reserve the heads and bones. Cut the fillets into small chunks. Shell half the prawns and reserve the trimmings to make the stock. Skin the white fish, discarding any bones, and cut into large chunks. Scrub the mussels well, discarding any open ones.

3 Put the fish trimmings and prawn trimmings in a pan with the onion and water. Bring the ingredients to the boil, then simmer gently for 30 minutes. Cool slightly and strain.

4 Soak the saffron in 15ml/ 1 tbsp boiling water. Heat 30ml/2 tbsp of the oil in a large sauté pan or flameproof casserole. Add the gurnard or mullet and white fish and fry over a high heat for 1 minute. Drain.

5 Heat the remaining oil and cook the fennel, garlic, orange rind and thyme until beginning to colour. Make up the strained stock to about 1.2 litres/2 pints/5 cups with water.

6 If using fresh tomatoes, plunge them into boiling water for 30 seconds, then refresh in cold water. Peel and chop. Add the stock to the pan with the saffron, tomatoes, tomato purée and bay leaves. Season, bring almost to the boil, then simmer gently, covered, for 20 minutes.

7 Stir in the gurnard or mullet, white fish, shelled and non-shelled prawns and add the mussels. Cover the pan and cook for 3–4 minutes. Discard any mussels that do not open. Serve the soup hot with the *rouille*.

Clam and Corn Chowder

Canned or bottled clams in brine, once drained, can be used as an alternative to fresh ones in their shells. Discard any clam shells that remain closed during cooking as this means they are already dead.

INGREDIENTS

Serves 4

300ml/½ pint/1¼ cups double (heavy) cream

75g/3oz/6 tbsp unsalted (sweet) butter

1 small onion, finely chopped

1 apple, cored and sliced

1 garlic clove, crushed

45ml/3 tbsp mild curry powder

350g/12oz/3 cups baby corn

225g/8oz cooked new potatoes

24 boiled baby (pearl) onions

600ml/1 pint/2½ cups fish stock

40 small clams

salt and freshly ground black pepper

8 lime wedges, to garnish (optional)

3 In another pan, melt the remaining butter and add the baby corn, potatoes and baby onions. Cook for 5 minutes. Increase the heat and add the cream mixture and stock. Bring to the boil.

4 Add the clams. Cover and cook until the clams have opened. Discard any that do not open. Season well to taste with salt and freshly ground black pepper and serve, garnished with lime wedges, if liked.

1 Pour the cream into a small pan and cook over a high heat until it is reduced by half.

2 In a larger pan, melt half the butter. Add the onion, apple, garlic and curry powder. Sauté until the onion is translucent. Add the reduced cream and stir well.

Clam and Basil Soup

Subtly sweet and spicy, this soup is an ideal appetizer for serving as part of a celebration dinner.

INGREDIENTS

Serves 4–6

30ml/2 tbsp olive oil

1 medium onion, finely chopped

leaves from 1 fresh or dried sprig of
   thyme, chopped or crumbled

2 garlic cloves, crushed

5–6 fresh basil leaves, plus extra to garnish

1.5–2.5ml/¼–½ tsp crushed red chillies,
   to taste

1 litre/1¾ pints/4 cups fish stock

350ml/12fl oz/1½ cups passata (bottled
   strained tomatoes)

5ml/1 tsp granulated sugar

90g/3½oz/scant 1 cup frozen peas

65g/2½oz/⅔ cup small pasta shapes, such
   as chifferini

225g/8oz frozen shelled clams

salt and freshly ground black pepper

1 Heat the oil in a large pan, add the finely chopped onion and cook gently for about 5 minutes until softened but not coloured. Add the thyme, then stir in the garlic, basil leaves and chillies.

2 Add the stock, passata and sugar to the pan, with salt and pepper to taste. Bring to the boil, then lower the heat and simmer gently for 15 minutes, stirring from time to time. Add the frozen peas and cook for a further 5 minutes.

3 Add the pasta to the stock mixture and bring to the boil, stirring. Lower the heat and simmer for about 5 minutes or according to the packet instructions, stirring frequently, until the pasta is *al dente.*

4 Turn the heat down to low, add the frozen clams and heat through for 2–3 minutes. Taste and adjust the seasoning. Serve hot in warmed bowls, garnished with basil leaves.

COOK'S TIP

Frozen shelled clams are available at good fishmongers and supermarkets. If you can't get them, use bottled or canned clams in natural juice (not vinegar). Italian delicatessens sell jars of clams in their shells. These both look and taste delicious and are not too expensive. For a special occasion, stir some into the soup.

Lamb, Bean and Pumpkin Soup

This is a hearty soup to warm the cockles of the heart in even the chilliest weather.

INGREDIENTS

Serves 4

115g/4oz/⅔ cup split black-eyed beans (pea), soaked for 2 hours or overnight

675g/1½lb neck (shoulder) of lamb, cut into medium-size chunks

5ml/1 tsp chopped fresh thyme

2 bay leaves

1.2 litres/2 pints/5 cups stock or water

1 onion, sliced

225g/8oz pumpkin, diced

2 black cardamom pods

7.5ml/1½ tsp ground turmeric

15ml/1 tbsp chopped fresh coriander (cilantro)

2.5ml/½ tsp caraway seeds

1 fresh green chilli, seeded and chopped

2 green bananas

1 carrot

salt and freshly ground black pepper

1 Drain the black-eyed beans, place them in a pan and cover with fresh cold water.

2 Bring the beans to the boil, boil rapidly for 10 minutes and then reduce the heat and simmer, covered, for about 40–50 minutes until tender, adding more water if necessary. Remove the pan from the heat and set aside to cool.

3 Meanwhile, put the lamb in a large pan, add the thyme, bay leaves and stock or water and bring to the boil. Cover and simmer over a moderate heat for 1 hour until tender.

4 Add the onion, pumpkin, cardamoms, turmeric, coriander, caraway, chilli and seasoning and stir. Bring back to a simmer and cook, uncovered, for 15 minutes, stirring occasionally, until the pumpkin is tender.

5 When the beans are cool, spoon into a blender or food processor with their liquid and blend to a smooth purée.

6 Peel the bananas and cut into medium slices. Cut the carrot into thin slices. Stir into the soup with the beans and cook for 10–12 minutes, until the carrot is tender. Adjust the seasoning and serve immediately.

Pork and Pickled Mustard Greens Soup

This highly flavoured soup makes an interesting start to a meal.

INGREDIENTS

Serves 4–6

225g/8oz pickled mustard leaves, soaked

50g/2oz cellophane noodles, soaked

15ml/1 tbsp vegetable oil

4 garlic cloves, finely sliced

1 litre/1¾ pints/4 cups chicken stock

450g/1lb pork ribs, cut into large chunks

30ml/2 tbsp fish sauce

a pinch of sugar

freshly ground black pepper

2 fresh red chillies, seeded and finely
    sliced, to garnish

1 Cut the pickled mustard leaves into bitesize pieces. Taste to check the seasoning. If they are too salty, soak them for a little longer.

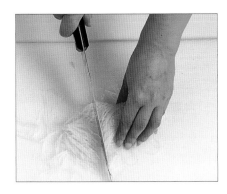

2 Drain the cellophane noodles, discarding the soaking water, and cut them into pieces about 5cm/2in long.

3 Heat the oil in a small frying pan, add the garlic and stir-fry until golden. Transfer to a bowl and set aside.

4 Put the stock in a pan, bring to the boil, then add the pork ribs and simmer gently for 10–15 minutes.

5 Add the pickled mustard leaves and cellophane noodles. Bring back to the boil. Season to taste with fish sauce, sugar and freshly ground black pepper.

6 Pour the soup into individual serving bowls. Garnish with the fried garlic and the red chillies and serve hot.

WINTER
WARMING SOUPS

V

Borscht

A simply stunning colour, this classic Russian soup is the perfect dish to serve when you want to offer something a little different.

INGREDIENTS

Serves 6

1 onion, chopped

450g/1lb raw beetroot (beet), peeled and chopped

2 celery sticks, chopped

½ red (bell) pepper, chopped

115g/4oz mushrooms, chopped

1 large cooking apple, chopped

25g/1oz/2 tbsp butter

30ml/2 tbsp sunflower oil

2 litres/3½ pints/9 cups stock or water

5ml/1 tsp cumin seeds

a pinch of dried thyme

1 large bay leaf

fresh lemon juice

salt and freshly ground black pepper

For the garnish

150ml/¼ pint/⅔ cup sour cream

a few sprigs of fresh dill

COOK'S TIP

The flavour of this marvellous soup matures and improves if it is made the day before it is needed.

1 Place the chopped vegetables and apple in a large pan with the butter, oil and 45ml/3 tbsp of the stock or water. Cover and cook gently for about 15 minutes, shaking the pan occasionally.

2 Stir in the cumin seeds and cook for 1 minute, then add the remaining stock or water, the thyme, bay leaf, lemon juice and seasoning to taste.

3 Bring the mixture to the boil, then cover the pan and turn down the heat to a gentle simmer. Cook for about 30 minutes.

4 Strain the vegetables and reserve the liquid. Process the vegetables in a food processor or blender until they are smooth and creamy.

5 Return the vegetables to the pan, add the reserved stock and reheat. Check the seasoning.

6 Divide into individual serving bowls. Garnish with swirls of sour cream in each bowl and top with a few sprigs of fresh dill.

Nettle Soup

A country-style soup which is a tasty variation of the classic Irish potato soup. Use wild nettles if you can find them, or a washed head of round lettuce if you prefer.

Serves 4

115g/4oz/¹/₂ cup butter
450g/1lb onions, sliced
450g/1lb potatoes, cut into chunks
750ml/1¹/₄ pints/3 cups chicken stock
25g/1oz nettle leaves
a small bunch of chives, chopped
salt and freshly ground black pepper
double (heavy) cream, to serve

2 Wearing rubber gloves, remove the nettle leaves from their stalks. Wash the leaves under cold running water, then dry on kitchen paper. Add to the pan and cook for a further 5 minutes.

3 Ladle the soup into a blender or food processor and process until smooth. Return to a clean pan and season well. Stir in the chives and serve with a swirl of cream and a sprinkling of pepper.

1 Melt the butter in a large pan and add the sliced onions. Cover and cook for about 5 minutes until just softened. Add the potatoes to the pan with the chicken stock. Cover and cook for 25 minutes.

COOK'S TIP

If you prefer, cut the vegetables finely and leave the cooked soup chunky rather than puréeing it.

Sweet Potato and Parsnip Soup

V

The sweetness of the two root vegetables comes through strongly in this delicious soup.

INGREDIENTS

Serves 6

15ml/1 tbsp sunflower oil

1 large leek, sliced

2 celery sticks, chopped

450g/1lb sweet potatoes, diced

225g/8oz/1½ cups parsnips, diced

900ml/1½ pints/3¾ cups
 vegetable stock

salt and freshly ground black pepper

For the garnish

15ml/1 tbsp chopped fresh parsley

roasted strips of sweet potatoes
 and parsnips

1 Heat the oil in a large pan and add the leek, celery, sweet potatoes and parsnips. Cook gently for about 5 minutes, stirring to prevent them browning or sticking to the pan.

2 Stir in the vegetable stock and bring to the boil, then cover and simmer gently for about 25 minutes, or until the vegetables are tender, stirring occasionally. Season to taste. Remove the pan from the heat and allow the soup to cool slightly.

3 Purée the soup in a blender or food processor until smooth, then return the soup to the pan and reheat gently. Ladle into warmed soup bowls to serve and sprinkle over the chopped parsley and roasted strips of sweet potatoes and parsnips.

V

Sweet Potato and Red Pepper Soup

As colourful as it is good to eat, this soup is a sure winner.

INGREDIENTS

Serves 6

2 red (bell) peppers (about 225g/8oz)
   seeded and cubed

500g/1¼lb sweet potatoes, cubed

1 onion, roughly chopped

2 large garlic cloves, roughly chopped

300ml/½ pint/1¼ cups dry white wine

1.2 litres/2 pints/5 cups
   vegetable stock

Tabasco sauce, to taste

salt and freshly ground black pepper

fresh country bread, to serve

1 Dice a small quantity of red pepper for the garnish and set aside. Put the rest into a pan with the cubed sweet potato, chopped onion and garlic, white wine and vegetable stock. Bring to the boil, lower the heat and simmer for 30 minutes or until all the vegetables are quite soft.

2 Transfer the mixture to a blender or food processor and process until smooth. Season to taste with salt, ground black pepper and a generous dash of Tabasco. Allow to cool slightly. Garnish with the reserved diced red pepper and serve warm or at room temperature.

Leek and Thyme Soup

*This is a filling soup, which can be
processed to a smooth purée or
served in its original peasant style.*

INGREDIENTS

Serves 4

900g/2lb leeks

450g/1lb potatoes

115g/4oz/½ cup butter

1 large sprig of fresh thyme, plus extra to
    garnish (optional)

300ml/½ pint/1¼ cups milk

salt and freshly ground black pepper

60ml/4 tbsp double (heavy) cream,
    to serve

1 Trim the leeks. If you are using
big winter leeks, strip away all
the coarse outer leaves, then cut
the leeks into thick slices. Wash the
leeks thoroughly under cold
running water.

2 Cut the potatoes into rough
dice, about 2.5cm/1in, and dry
on kitchen paper.

3 Melt the butter in a large pan
and add the leeks and 1 sprig
of thyme. Cover and cook for
4–5 minutes until softened. Add
the potato pieces and just enough
cold water to cover the vegetables.
Re-cover and cook over a low heat
for 30 minutes.

4 Pour in the milk and season
with salt and pepper. Cover and
simmer for a further 30 minutes.
You will find that some of the
potato breaks up, leaving you
with a semi-puréed and rather
lumpy soup.

5 Remove the sprig of thyme
(the leaves will have fallen into
the soup) and serve, adding 15ml/
1 tbsp cream and a garnish of
thyme to each portion, if using.

Green Pea Soup with Spinach

This lovely green soup was invented by the wife of a seventeenth-century British Member of Parliament, and it has stood the test of time.

INGREDIENTS

Serves 6

450g/1lb/generous 3 cups podded fresh or
    frozen peas
1 leek, finely sliced
2 garlic cloves, crushed
2 rindless back (lean) bacon rashers
    (strips), finely diced
1.2 litres/2 pints/5 cups ham stock
30ml/2 tbsp olive oil
50g/2oz fresh spinach, shredded
40g/1½oz/⅓ cup white cabbage,
    finely shredded
½ small lettuce, finely shredded
1 celery stick, finely chopped
a large handful of parsley, finely chopped
½ carton mustard and cress
20ml/4 tsp chopped fresh mint
a pinch of ground mace
salt and freshly ground black pepper

1 Put the peas, leek, garlic and bacon in a large pan. Add the stock, bring to the boil, then lower the heat and simmer for 20 minutes.

2 About 5 minutes before the pea mixture is ready, heat the oil in a deep frying pan.

3 Add the spinach, cabbage, lettuce, celery and herbs to the frying pan. Cover and sweat the mixture over a low heat until soft.

4 Transfer the pea mixture to a blender or food processor and process until smooth. Return to the clean pan, add the sweated vegetables and herbs and heat through. Season with mace, salt and pepper and serve.

French Onion Soup

In France, this standard bistro fare is served so frequently that it is simply referred to as gratinée.

INGREDIENTS

Serves 6–8

15g/¹/₂oz/l tbsp butter

30ml/2 tbsp olive oil

4 large onions, finely sliced

2–5 garlic cloves

5ml/1 tsp sugar

2.5ml/¹/₂ tsp dried thyme

30ml/2 tbsp plain (all-purpose) flour

120ml/4fl oz/¹/₂ cup dry white wine

2 litres/3¹/₂ pints/9 cups beef stock

30ml/2 tbsp brandy (optional)

6–8 thick slices French bread, toasted

350g/12oz/3 cups Gruyère or Emmenthal cheese, grated

1 In a large, heavy pan or flameproof casserole, heat the butter and oil over a medium-high heat. Add the onions and cook for 10–12 minutes until they are softened and beginning to brown.

2 Putting one garlic clove aside, finely chop the rest and add to the onions. Add the sugar and fresh thyme and cook over a medium heat for 30–35 minutes until the onions are well browned, stirring frequently.

3 Sprinkle over the flour and stir until well blended. Stir in the wine and stock and bring to the boil. Skim off any foam that rises to the surface, then reduce the heat and simmer gently for 45 minutes. Stir in the brandy, if using.

4 Preheat the grill (broiler). Rub each slice of toasted French bread with the remaining garlic clove. Place six or eight ovenproof soup bowls on a baking sheet and fill about three-quarters full with the onion soup.

5 Float a piece of toast in each bowl. Top with grated cheese, dividing it evenly, and grill (broil) about 15cm/6in from the heat for about 3–4 minutes until the cheese begins to melt and bubble. Serve piping hot.

V

Root Vegetable Soup

Simmer a selection of popular winter root vegetables together for a warming and satisfying soup. Its creamy taste comes from adding crème fraîche just before serving.

INGREDIENTS

Serves 6

3 medium carrots, chopped

1 large potato, chopped

1 large parsnip, chopped

1 large turnip or small swede
     (rutabaga), chopped

1 onion, chopped

30ml/2 tbsp sunflower oil

25g/1oz/2 tbsp butter

1.5 litres/2½ pints/6¼ cups water

1 piece fresh root ginger, peeled
     and grated

300ml/½ pint/1¼ cups milk

45ml/3 tbsp crème fraîche

30ml/2 tbsp chopped fresh dill

15ml/1 tbsp lemon juice

salt and freshly ground black pepper

sprigs of fresh dill, to garnish

1 Put the carrots, potato, parsnip, turnip or swede and onion into a large pan with the oil and butter. Fry lightly, then cover and sweat the vegetables on a low heat for 15 minutes, shaking the pan occasionally.

2 Pour in the water, bring to the boil and season well. Cover and simmer for 20 minutes until the vegetables are soft.

3 Strain the vegetables, reserving the stock, add the ginger and vegetables to a food processor or blender and purée until smooth. Return the puréed mixture and stock to the pan. Add the milk and stir while the soup gently reheats.

4 Remove from the heat and stir in the crème fraîche, plus the dill and lemon juice. Season if necessary. Reheat the soup but do not allow it to boil or it may curdle. Serve garnished with sprigs of fresh dill.

Pumpkin Soup

V

The sweet flavour of pumpkin is excellent in soups, teaming well with other savoury ingredients such as onions and potatoes to make a warm and comforting dish. For added flavour, try roasting the pumpkin chunks before adding to the soup with the stock.

INGREDIENTS

Serves 4–6

15ml/1 tbsp sunflower oil

25g/1oz/2 tbsp butter

1 large onion, sliced

675g/1½lb pumpkin, cut into
   large chunks

450g/1 1b potatoes, sliced

600ml/1 pint/2½ cups vegetable stock

a good pinch of freshly grated nutmeg

5ml/1 tsp chopped fresh tarragon

600ml/1 pint/2½ cups milk

about 5–10ml/1–2 tsp lemon juice

salt and freshly ground black pepper

1 Heat the oil and butter in a heavy pan and cook the onion for 4–5 minutes over a gentle heat until softened but not browned, stirring frequently.

2 Add the pumpkin and sliced potatoes, stir well, then cover and sweat over a low heat for about 10 minutes until the vegetables are almost tender, stirring occasionally to stop them sticking to the pan.

3 Stir in the stock, nutmeg, tarragon and seasoning. Bring to the boil and then simmer for about 10 minutes until the vegetables are completely tender.

4 Allow to cool slightly, then pour into a food processor or blender and process until smooth. Pour back into a clean pan and add the milk. Heat gently and then taste, adding the lemon juice and extra seasoning, if necessary. Serve piping hot.

Mushroom and Herb Potage

Do not worry if this soup is not completely smooth – a slightly nutty texture is especially nice.

INGREDIENTS

Serves 4

50g/2oz smoked streaky (fatty) bacon

1 onion, chopped

15ml/1 tbsp sunflower oil

350g/12oz open field (portabello)
   mushrooms or a mixture of wild and
   brown mushrooms

600ml/1 pint/2½ cups good meat stock

30ml/2 tbsp sweet sherry

30ml/2 tbsp chopped fresh mixed herbs,
   such as sage, rosemary, thyme and
   marjoram, or 10ml/2 tsp dried herbs

salt and freshly ground black pepper

a few sprigs of sage or marjoram,
   to garnish

60ml/4 tbsp thick Greek
   (US strained plain) yogurt, to serve

1 Roughly chop the bacon and place in a large pan. Cook gently until all the fat comes out of the bacon.

2 Add the onion and soften, adding oil if necessary. Wipe the mushrooms clean, roughly chop and add to the pan. Cover and sweat until they have completely softened and their liquid has run out.

3 Add the stock, sherry, herbs and seasoning, cover and simmer for 10–12 minutes. Process the soup in a food processor or blender until smooth, but don't worry if you still have a slightly textured result.

4 Check the seasoning and heat through. Serve with a spoon of yogurt and a sprig of fresh sage or marjoram in each bowl.

Split Pea and Pumpkin Soup

Salt (corned) beef is often used in this creamy pea soup. This is the vegetarian version, however.

INGREDIENTS

Serves 4

225g/8oz/1 cup split peas
1.2 litres/2 pints/5 cups water
25g/1oz/2 tbsp butter
1 onion, finely chopped
225g/8oz pumpkin, chopped
3 tomatoes, peeled and chopped
5ml/1 tsp dried tarragon, crushed
15ml/1 tbsp chopped fresh coriander
    (cilantro), plus extra to garnish
2.5ml/$\frac{1}{2}$ tsp ground cumin
1 vegetable stock (bouillon) cube
chilli powder, to taste

1 Soak the split peas overnight in enough water to cover them completely, then drain. Place the split peas in a large pan, add the water and boil for about 30 minutes until tender.

2 In a separate pan, melt the butter and sauté the onion until soft but not browned.

3 Add the pumpkin, tomatoes, tarragon, coriander, cumin, cube and chilli powder to the pan. Crumble the stock cube into the mixture and, on a high heat, bring to the boil.

4 Stir the vegetable mixture into the cooked split peas and their liquid. Simmer gently for about 20 minutes or until the vegetables are tender. If the soup is too thick, add another 150ml/$\frac{1}{4}$ pint/$\frac{2}{3}$ cup water. Serve hot, garnished with sprigs of coriander.

Garcia and Lentil Soup

High in fibre, lentils make a particularly tasty soup. Unlike many pulses, they do not need to be soaked before being cooked.

INGREDIENTS

Serves 6

225g/8oz/1 cup red lentils, rinsed
   and drained

2 onions, finely chopped

2 large garlic cloves, finely chopped

1 carrot, finely chopped

30ml/2 tbsp olive oil

2 bay leaves

a generous pinch of dried marjoram
   or oregano

1.5 litres/2½ pints/6¼ cups
   vegetable stock

30ml/2 tbsp red wine vinegar

salt and freshly ground black pepper

celery leaves, to garnish

crusty bread rolls, to serve

1 Put all the ingredients except for the vinegar, seasoning and garnish in a large, heavy pan. Bring the ingredients to the boil over a medium heat, then lower the heat and simmer for 1½ hours, stirring the soup occasionally to prevent the lentils from sticking to the bottom of the pan.

2 Remove the bay leaves and add the red wine vinegar. Season with salt and ground black pepper to taste. If the soup is too thick, thin it with a little extra vegetable stock or water. Serve the soup in heated bowls, garnished with celery leaves. Serve with warmed crusty bread rolls.

COOK'S TIP

If you buy your lentils loose, remember to tip them into a sieve or colander and pick them over, removing any pieces of grit, before rinsing them.

Lamb and Lentil Soup

Lamb and lentils go together so well, they seem to have been made for one another.

INGREDIENTS

Serves 4

about 1.5 litres/2½ pints/6¼ cups water or stock

900g/2lb neck (shoulder) of lamb, cut into chops

½ onion, chopped

1 garlic clove, crushed

1 bay leaf

1 clove

2 sprigs of fresh thyme

225g/8oz potatoes, cut into 2.5cm/1in dice

175g/6oz/¾ cup red lentils

salt and freshly ground black pepper

chopped fresh parsley

1 Put about 1.2 litres/2 pints / 5 cups of the stock or water and the meat in a large pan with the onion, garlic, bay leaf, clove and sprigs of thyme. Bring to the boil and simmer for about 1 hour until the lamb is tender.

COOK'S TIP

Red lentils do not need soaking before they are cooked; simply pick them over and remove any pieces of grit and debris, then rinse well.

2 Add the pieces of potato and the lentils to the pan and season the soup with a little salt and plenty of black pepper. Add the remaining stock or water to come just above the surface of the meat and vegetables; you may need more if the soup becomes too thick during cooking.

3 Cover and simmer for 25 minutes or until the lentils are cooked and well blended into the soup. Taste the soup and adjust the seasoning as necessary. Stir in the parsley and serve.

Tomato and Vermicelli Soup

The vermicelli is lightly fried before being simmered in this tasty soup.

INGREDIENTS

Serves 4

30ml/2 tbsp olive or corn oil

50g/2oz/⅓ cup vermicelli

1 onion, roughly chopped

1 garlic clove, chopped

450g/1lb tomatoes, peeled, seeded and
  roughly chopped

1 litre/1¾ pints/4 cups chicken stock

1.5ml/¼ tsp sugar

15ml/1 tbsp finely chopped fresh
  coriander (cilantro), plus extra
  to garnish

salt and freshly ground black pepper

25g/1oz/⅓ cup grated Parmesan cheese,
  to serve

1 Heat the oil in a frying pan and sauté the vermicelli over a moderate heat until it is golden brown. Take care not to let the strands burn.

2 Remove the pan from the heat. Lift out the vermicelli with a slotted spoon, drain on kitchen paper and set aside.

3 Purée the onion, garlic and tomatoes in a food processor until smooth. Return the frying pan to the heat. When the oil is hot, add the purée. Cook, stirring constantly, for about 5 minutes or until thick.

4 Transfer the purée to a pan. Add the vermicelli and pour in the stock. Season with sugar, salt and pepper. Stir in 15ml/1 tbsp coriander, bring to the boil, then lower the heat, cover the pan and simmer the soup until the vermicelli is tender.

5 Serve in heated bowls, sprinkle with chopped fresh coriander, and offer the Parmesan separately.

Lightly Spiced Tomato Soup

Simple and quick to make, this tomato soup will soon become one of your firm favourites.

INGREDIENTS

Serves 4

15ml/1 tbsp corn or groundnut
  (peanut) oil

1 onion, finely chopped

900g/2lb tomatoes, peeled, seeded
  and chopped

475ml/16fl oz/2 cups chicken stock

2 large sprigs of fresh coriander (cilantro)

salt and freshly ground black pepper

coarsely ground black pepper, to serve

1 Heat the oil in a large pan and gently cook the onion, stirring frequently, for about 5 minutes until it is soft and transparent but not brown.

2 Add the chopped tomatoes, chicken stock and coriander to the pan. Bring to the boil, then lower the heat, cover the pan and simmer gently for 15 minutes or until the tomatoes are soft.

3 Remove and discard the coriander. Press the soup through a sieve and return it to the clean pan. Season and heat through. Serve sprinkled with coarsely ground black pepper.

Broccoli and Bread Soup

Broccoli grows abundantly around Rome and is served in this soup with garlic toasts.

INGREDIENTS

Serves 6

675g/1½lb broccoli spears

1.75 litres/3 pints/7½ cups chicken or vegetable stock

15ml/1 tbsp lemon juice

salt and freshly ground black pepper

To serve

6 slices white bread

1 large garlic clove, cut in half

grated Parmesan cheese (optional)

1 Using a small, sharp knife, peel the broccoli stems, starting from the base and pulling gently up towards the florets. (The peel should come off easily.) Chop the broccoli into small chunks.

2 Bring the stock to the boil in a large pan. Add the broccoli and simmer for about 10 minutes until soft.

3 Purée about half of the soup and mix into the rest of the soup. Season with salt, pepper and lemon juice.

4 Reheat the soup. Toast the bread, rub with garlic and cut into quarters. Place 3 or 4 pieces of toast in the bottom of each soup plate. Ladle on the soup. Serve at once, with Parmesan if liked.

Tomato and Bread Soup

This colourful Florentine recipe was created to use up stale bread. It can be made with very ripe fresh or canned plum tomatoes.

INGREDIENTS

Serves 4

90ml/6 tbsp olive oil

small piece dried chilli, crumbled (optional)

175g/6oz/1½ cups stale bread, cut into 2.5cm/1in cubes

1 medium onion, finely chopped

2 garlic cloves, finely chopped

675g/1½lb ripe tomatoes, peeled and chopped, or 2 x 400g/14oz cans peeled plum tomatoes, chopped

45ml/3 tbsp chopped fresh basil

1.5 litres/2½ pints/6¼ cups light meat stock or water, or a combination of both

salt and freshly ground black pepper

extra virgin olive oil, to serve (optional)

1 Heat 60ml/4 tbsp of the oil in a large pan. Add the chilli, if using, and stir for 1–2 minutes. Add the bread cubes and cook until golden, then remove to a plate and drain on kitchen paper.

2 Add the remaining oil, the onion and garlic to the pan and cook until the onion softens. Stir in the tomatoes, basil and the reserved bread cubes. Season with salt. Cook over a moderate heat, stirring occasionally, for about 15 minutes.

3 Meanwhile, heat the stock or water to simmering. Add it to the tomato mixture and stir well. Bring to the boil. Lower the heat slightly and simmer for 20 minutes.

4 Remove the soup from the heat. Use a fork to mash together the tomatoes and bread. Season with pepper, and more salt if necessary. Allow to stand for 10 minutes. Just before serving, swirl in a little extra virgin olive oil, if liked.

Spanish Garlic Soup

This is a simple and satisfying soup, made with garlic, which is one of the most popular ingredients in the quick cook's kitchen.

INGREDIENTS

Serves 4

30ml/2 tbsp olive oil

4 large garlic cloves, peeled

4 slices French bread, about
    5mm/¼in thick

15ml/1 tbsp paprika

1 litre/1¾ pints/4 cups beef stock

1.5ml/¼ tsp ground cumin

a pinch of saffron threads

4 eggs

salt and freshly ground black pepper

chopped fresh parsley, to garnish

1 Preheat the oven to 230°C/
450°F/Gas 8. Heat the oil in a
large pan. Add the whole garlic
cloves and cook until golden.
Remove and set aside. Fry the bread
in the oil until golden, then set aside.

COOK'S TIP
~

When you switch on the oven,
put a baking sheet in at the same
time. Stand the soup bowls on
the hot baking sheet when you
put them in the oven and you
will be able to remove them
easily when the eggs are set.

---

2 Add the paprika to the pan,
and cook for a few seconds.
Stir in the beef stock, cumin and
saffron, then add the reserved
garlic, crushing the cloves with the
back of a wooden spoon. Season
with salt and pepper, then cook for
about 5 minutes.

3 Ladle the soup into four
ovenproof bowls and break
1 egg into each one. Place a slice
of fried bread on top of each egg,
then put the bowls in the oven for
about 3–4 minutes, until the eggs
are set. Sprinkle each portion with
parsley and serve at once.

Beetroot and Butter Bean Soup

This soup is a simplified version of borscht and is prepared in a fraction of the time. Serve with a spoonful of sour cream and a scattering of chopped fresh parsley.

INGREDIENTS

Serves 4

30ml/2 tbsp vegetable oil

1 medium onion, sliced

5ml/l tsp caraway seeds

finely grated rind of ½ orange

250g/9oz cooked beetroot (beet), grated

1.2 litres/2 pints/5 cups beef stock
   or rassol (see Cook's Tip)

400g/14oz can butter (lima) beans,
   drained and rinsed

15ml/1 tbsp wine vinegar

60ml/4 tbsp sour cream

60ml/4 tbsp chopped fresh parsley,
   to garnish

1 Heat the oil in a large pan and cook the onion, caraway seeds and orange rind until softened but not coloured.

2 Add the beetroot, stock or rassol, butter beans and vinegar and simmer over a low heat for a further 10 minutes.

3 Divide the soup between four bowls, add a spoonful of sour cream to each, sprinkle with chopped parsley and serve.

COOK'S TIP

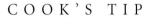

Rassol is a beetroot (beet) broth, which is used to impart a strong beetroot colour and flavour. You are most likely to find it in Kosher food stores.

Winter Vegetable Soup

No fewer than eight varieties of vegetables are packed into this hearty and nutritious soup.

INGREDIENTS

Serves 8

1 medium Savoy cabbage, quartered
 and cored
30ml/2 tbsp corn oil
4 carrots, finely sliced
2 celery stalks, finely sliced
2 parsnips, diced
1.5 litres/2½ pints/6¼ cups chicken stock
3 medium potatoes, diced
2 courgettes (zucchini), sliced
1 small red (bell) pepper, seeded and diced
115g/4oz/2 cups cauliflower florets
2 tomatoes, seeded and diced
2.5ml/½ tsp fresh thyme leaves or
 ¼ tsp dried thyme
30ml/2 tbsp chopped fresh parsley
salt and freshly ground black pepper

1 Using a sharp knife, slice the cabbage quarters into thin strips across the leaves.

2 Heat the oil in a large pan. Add the cabbage, carrots, celery and parsnips and cook for 10–15 minutes over medium heat, stirring frequently.

3 Stir the stock into the vegetables and bring to the boil, skimming off any foam that rises to the surface.

4 Add the potatoes, courgettes, pepper, cauliflower and tomatoes with the herbs, and salt and pepper to taste. Bring back to the boil. Reduce the heat to low, cover the pan and simmer for 15–20 minutes until the vegetables are tender. Serve hot.

Onion and Pancetta Soup

This warming winter soup comes from Umbria, where it is sometimes thickened with beaten eggs and plenty of grated Parmesan cheese. It is then served on top of hot toasted croûtes – rather like savoury scrambled eggs.

INGREDIENTS

Serves 4

115g/4oz pancetta rashers (strips), rinds removed, roughly chopped

30ml/2 tbsp olive oil

15g/½oz/1 tbsp butter

675g/1½lb onions, finely sliced

10ml/2 tsp granulated sugar

about 1.2 litres/2 pints/5 cups chicken stock

350g/12oz ripe Italian plum tomatoes, peeled and roughly chopped

a few fresh basil leaves, shredded

salt and freshly ground black pepper

grated Parmesan cheese, to serve

1 Put the chopped pancetta in a large pan and heat gently, stirring constantly, until the fat runs. Increase the heat to medium, add the oil, butter, sliced onions and sugar and stir well to mix.

2 Half-cover the pan and cook the onions gently for about 20 minutes until golden. Stir frequently and lower the heat if necessary.

3 Add the stock, tomatoes and salt and pepper and bring to the boil, stirring. Lower the heat, half-cover the pan and simmer, stirring occasionally, for about 30 minutes.

4 Check the consistency of the soup and add a little more stock or water if it is too thick.

5 Just before serving, stir in most of the basil and adjust the seasoning to taste. Serve hot, garnished with the remaining shredded basil. Hand round the freshly grated Parmesan separately.

COOK'S TIP

Look for Vidalia onions to make this soup. They are available at large supermarkets, and have a sweet flavour and attractive, yellowish flesh.

Cauliflower, Flageolet and Fennel Seed Soup

The sweet, anise-liquorice flavour of the fennel seeds gives a delicious edge to this hearty soup.

INGREDIENTS

Serves 4–6

15ml/1 tbsp olive oil

1 garlic clove, crushed

1 onion, chopped

10ml/2 tsp fennel seeds

1 cauliflower, cut into small florets

2 x 400g/14oz cans flageolet (small cannellini) beans, drained and rinsed

1.2 litres/2 pints/5 cups vegetable stock or water

salt and freshly ground black pepper

chopped fresh parsley, to garnish

toasted slices of French bread, to serve

3 Bring the vegetable mixture to the boil. Reduce the heat and simmer gently for about 10 minutes or until the cauliflower is tender. Pour the soup mixture into a blender or food processor and blend until smooth.

4 Stir in the remaining beans and season to taste. Reheat and pour into bowls. Sprinkle with chopped parsley and serve with toasted slices of French bread.

1 Heat the olive oil. Add the garlic, onion and fennel seeds and cook gently for 5 minutes or until softened.

2 Add the cauliflower florets, half the beans and the vegetable stock or water.

Yellow Broth

This is one of many versions of this famous Northern Irish soup, which is both thickened with, and given its flavour by, oatmeal.

Serves 4

25g/1oz/2 tbsp butter

1 onion, finely chopped

1 celery stick, finely chopped

1 carrot, finely chopped

25g/1oz/¼ cup plain (all-purpose) flour

900ml/1½ pints/3¾ cups chicken stock

25g/1oz/¼ cup medium oatmeal

115g/4oz spinach, chopped

30ml/2 tbsp single (light) cream

salt and freshly ground black pepper

chopped fresh parsley, to
   garnish (optional)

1 Melt the butter in a large pan. Add the onion, celery and carrot and cook, stirring occasionally, for about 2 minutes until they begin to soften.

2 Stir in the flour and cook gently for a further 1 minute, stirring constantly. Pour in the chicken stock, bring to the boil and cover. Reduce the heat and simmer for 30 minutes until the vegetables are tender.

3 Stir in the oatmeal and chopped spinach and cook for a further 15 minutes, stirring from time to time.

4 Stir in the cream and season well. Serve garnished with chopped fresh parsley, if using.

Corn and Crab Meat Soup

This soup originated in the USA but it has since been introduced into China. You must use creamed sweetcorn for the right consistency.

INGREDIENTS

Serves 4

115g/4oz crab meat

2.5ml/½ tsp finely chopped fresh
   root ginger

30ml/2 tbsp milk

15ml/1 tbsp cornflour (cornstarch)

2 egg whites

600ml/1 pint/2½ cups vegetable stock

225g/8oz can creamed sweetcorn

salt and freshly ground black pepper

chopped spring onions (scallions),
   to garnish

3 In a wok or large pan, bring the vegetable stock gently to the boil. Add the creamed sweetcorn and bring back to the boil once more.

4 Stir in the crab meat and egg white mixture. Season to taste with salt and ground black pepper and stir gently until well blended. Serve garnished with chopped spring onions.

1 Flake the crab meat and mix with the ginger in a bowl. In another bowl, mix the milk and cornflour until smooth.

2 Beat the egg whites until frothy, add the milk and cornflour mixture and beat again until smooth. Blend with the crab meat.

VARIATION

If you prefer, you can use a coarsely chopped chicken breast portion instead of crab meat.

Vegetable and Herb Chowder

V

A medley of fresh vegetables and herbs combines to make a delicious lunchtime soup.

INGREDIENTS

Serves 4

25g/1oz/2 tbsp butter
1 onion, finely chopped
1 leek, finely sliced
1 celery stalk, diced
1 yellow (bell) pepper, seeded and diced
30ml/2 tbsp chopped fresh parsley
15ml/1 tbsp plain (all-purpose) flour
1.2 litres/2 pints/5 cups vegetable stock
350g/12oz potatoes, diced
a few sprigs of fresh thyme or 2.5ml/
    ½ tsp dried thyme
1 bay leaf
115g/4oz/1 cup young runner (green)
    beans, thinly sliced on the diagonal
120ml/4fl oz/½ cup milk
salt and freshly ground black pepper

1 Melt the butter in a heavy pan or flameproof casserole and add the onion, leek, celery, yellow pepper and parsley. Cover and cook gently over low heat until the vegetables are soft.

2 Add the flour and stir until well blended. Slowly add the stock, stirring to combine. Bring to the boil, stirring frequently.

3 Add the potatoes, thyme and bay leaf. Simmer, uncovered, for about 10 minutes.

4 Add the beans and simmer for a further 10–15 minutes until all the vegetables are tender.

5 Stir in the milk. Season with salt and pepper. Heat through. Before serving, discard the thyme stalks and bay leaf. Serve hot.

Creamy Cod Chowder

The sharp flavour of the smoked cod contrasts well with the creamy soup. Serve this soup as a substantial appetizer before a light main course. Warm, crusty wholemeal (whole-wheat) bread goes well with it.

INGREDIENTS

Serves 4–6

350g/12oz smoked cod fillet
1 small onion, finely chopped
1 bay leaf
4 black peppercorns
900ml/1½ pints/3¾ cups milk
10ml/2 tsp cornflour (cornstarch)
10ml/2 tsp cold water
200g/7oz can sweetcorn kernels
15ml/1 tbsp chopped fresh parsley
crusty wholemeal (wholewheat) bread,
    to serve

COOK'S TIP

The flavour of the chowder improves if it is made a day in advance. Chill in the refrigerator until required, then reheat gently to prevent the fish from disintegrating.

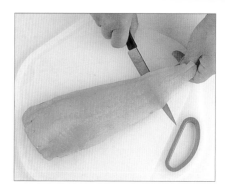

1 Skin the fish with a knife and put into a large pan with the onion, bay leaf, black peppercorns and milk.

2 Bring to the boil. Reduce the heat and simmer very gently for 12–15 minutes, or until the fish is just cooked. Do not overcook.

3 Using a slotted spoon, lift out the fish and flake into large chunks. Remove and discard the bay leaf and peppercorns.

4 Blend the cornflour with the water until it forms a smooth paste, and add to the pan with the rest of the ingredients. Bring to the boil and simmer for 1 minute or until slightly thickened.

5 Drain the sweetcorn kernels and add to the pan together with the flaked fish and chopped fresh parsley.

6 Reheat the soup until piping hot, but do not boil, taking care that the fish does not disintegrate. Ladle into soup bowls and serve straight away with plenty of warm wholemeal bread.

Salmon Chowder

Dill is the perfect partner for salmon in this creamy soup.

Serves 4

20g/³⁄₄oz/1¹⁄₂ tbsp butter or margarine

1 onion, finely chopped

1 leek, finely chopped

1 small fennel bulb, finely chopped

25g/1oz/¹⁄₄ cup plain (all-purpose) flour

1.75 litres/3 pints/7¹⁄₂ cups fish stock

2 medium potatoes, cut in 1 cm/¹⁄₂ in cubes

450g/1lb boneless, skinless salmon, cut in
   2cm/³⁄₄in cubes

175ml/6fl oz/³⁄₄ cup milk

120ml/4fl oz/¹⁄₂ cup whipping cream

30ml/2 tbsp chopped fresh dill

salt and freshly ground black pepper

1 Melt the butter or margarine in a large pan. Add the onion, leek and chopped fennel and cook over a medium heat for 5–8 minutes until softened, stirring from time to time.

2 Stir in the flour. Reduce the heat to low and cook for 3 minutes, stirring occasionally.

3 Add the fish stock and potatoes. Season with salt and ground black pepper. Bring to the boil, then reduce the heat, cover and simmer for about 20 minutes or until the potatoes are tender.

4 Add the salmon and simmer gently for 3–5 minutes until it is just cooked.

5 Stir in the milk, cream, and dill. Cook until just warmed through, but do not boil. Adjust the seasoning and then serve.

Smoked Haddock and Potato Soup

The proper name for this traditional Scottish soup is cullen skink. *A* cullen *is the seatown or port district of a town, while* skink *means stock or broth.*

INGREDIENTS

Serves 6

1 smoked haddock, about 350g/12oz

1 onion, chopped

1 bouquet garni

900ml/1½ pints/3¾ cups water

500g/1¼lb potatoes, quartered

600ml/1 pint/2½ cups milk

40g/1½oz/3 tbsp butter

salt and freshly ground black pepper

chopped fresh chives, to garnish

crusty bread, to serve

1 Put the haddock, onion, bouquet garni and water into a large pan and bring to the boil. Skim the scum from the surface, then cover the pan. Reduce the heat and poach for 10–15 minutes, until the haddock flakes easily.

2 Lift the haddock from the pan, using a metal spatula, and remove the skin and bones. Flake the flesh and reserve. Return the skin and bones to the pan and simmer, uncovered, for about 30 minutes. Strain the stock.

3 Return the stock to the pan, then add the potatoes and simmer for about 25 minutes, or until tender. Remove the potatoes from the pan using a slotted spoon. Add the milk to the pan and bring to the boil.

4 Meanwhile, mash the potatoes with the butter, then whisk into the liquid in the pan until thick and creamy. Add the flaked fish to the pan and adjust the seasoning. Sprinkle with chives and serve at once with crusty bread.

SPECIAL
OCCASION
SOUPS

Butternut Squash Bisque

This is a fragrant, creamy and delicately flavoured soup.

INGREDIENTS

Serves 4

25g/1oz/2 tbsp butter or margarine

2 small onions, finely chopped

450g/1lb butternut squash, peeled, seeded and cubed

1.2 litres/2 pints/5 cups chicken stock

225g/8oz potatoes, cubed

5ml/1 tsp paprika

120ml/4fl oz/½ cup whipping cream (optional)

25ml/1½ tbsp chopped fresh chives, plus a few whole chives to garnish

salt and freshly ground black pepper

1 Melt the butter or margarine in a large pan. Add the onions and cook for about 5 minutes until soft but not browned.

2 Add the squash, stock, potatoes and paprika. Bring to the boil. Reduce the heat to low, cover the pan and simmer for about 35 minutes until all the vegetables are soft.

3 Pour the soup into a food processor or blender and process until smooth. Return the soup to the pan and stir in the cream, if using. Season with salt and pepper. Reheat gently.

4 Stir in the chopped chives just before serving. Garnish each serving with a few whole chives.

Red Onion and Beetroot Soup

V

This beautiful, ruby-red soup, with its contrasting swirl of yogurt, will look stunning at any dinner party.

INGREDIENTS

Serves 4–6

15ml/1 tbsp olive oil

350g/12oz red onions, sliced

2 garlic cloves, crushed

275g/10oz cooked beetroot (beet), cut into sticks

1.2 litres/2 pints/5 cups vegetable stock or water

50g/2oz/1 cup cooked soup pasta

30ml/2 tbsp raspberry vinegar

salt and freshly ground black pepper

natural (plain) yogurt or fromage blanc and chopped fresh chives, to garnish

2 Cook the ingredients gently for about 20 minutes or until they are soft and tender, stirring occasionally to stop them from sticking to the bottom of the pan.

3 Add the beetroot, stock or water, cooked pasta and vinegar and heat through. Season and garnish with swirls of yogurt or fromage blanc and chives.

1 Heat the olive oil in a large saucepan or flameproof casserole and add the onions and garlic.

COOK'S TIP
◞

Try substituting cooked barley for the pasta to give extra nuttiness to the flavour.

Beetroot Soup with Ravioli

Beetroot (beet) and pasta make an unusual combination, but this soup is no less good for that.

INGREDIENTS

Serves 4–6

1 quantity of Basic Pasta Dough (*see page 112*)

1 egg white, beaten, for brushing

flour, for dusting

1 small onion or shallot, finely chopped

2 garlic cloves, crushed

5ml/1 tsp fennel seeds

600ml/1 pint/2½ cups chicken or vegetable stock

225g/8oz cooked beetroot (beet)

30ml/2 tbsp fresh orange juice

fresh fennel or dill leaves, to garnish

crusty bread, to serve

For the filling

115g/4oz mushrooms, finely chopped

1 shallot or small onion, finely chopped

1–2 garlic cloves, crushed

5ml/1 tsp chopped fresh thyme

15ml/1 tbsp chopped fresh parsley

90ml/6 tbsp fresh white breadcrumbs

salt and freshly ground black pepper

a large pinch of freshly grated nutmeg

1 Put all the filling ingredients in a food processor or blender and process to a paste.

2 Roll the pasta into thin sheets. Lay one piece over a ravioli tray and put 5ml/1 tsp of the filling into each depression. Brush around the edges of each ravioli with egg white. Cover with another sheet of pasta and press the edges together well to seal. Transfer to a floured dishtowel and rest for 1 hour before cooking.

3 Cook the ravioli in boiling, salted water for 2 minutes. (Cook in batches to stop them sticking together.) Remove and drop into a bowl of cold water for 5 seconds before placing on a tray. (You can make these pasta shapes a day in advance and store in the refrigerator.)

4 Put the onion, garlic and fennel seeds into a pan with 150ml/¼ pint/⅔ cup of the stock. Bring to the boil, cover and simmer for 5 minutes. Peel and dice the beetroot, reserving 60ml/4 tbsp for the garnish. Add the rest to the soup with the remaining stock, and bring to the boil.

5 Add the orange juice and cooked ravioli and simmer for 2 minutes. Serve in shallow soup bowls, garnished with the reserved diced beetroot and fresh fennel or dill leaves. Serve hot, with crusty bread.

Italian Vegetable Soup

V

*The success of this clear soup
depends on the quality of the stock,
so use home-made vegetable stock
rather than stock (bouillon) cubes.*

INGREDIENTS

Serves 4

1 small carrot
l baby leek
1 celery stick
50g/2oz green cabbage
900ml/1½ pints/3¾ cups vegetable stock
1 bay leaf
115g/4oz/1 cup cooked cannellini beans
25g/1oz/¼ cup soup pasta, such as tiny
   shells, bows, stars or elbows
salt and freshly ground black pepper
chopped fresh chives, to garnish

1 Cut the carrot, leek and celery into 5cm/2in long julienne strips. Finely shred the cabbage.

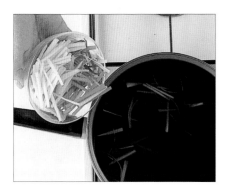

2 Put the stock and bay leaf into a large pan and bring to the boil. Add the carrot, leek and celery, cover and simmer for 6 minutes, until the vegetables are softened, but not tender.

3 Add the cabbage, beans and pasta, then simmer, uncovered, for a further 4–5 minutes, or until the vegetables are tender and the pasta is *al dente*.

4 Remove the bay leaf and season to taste. Ladle the soup into four warmed soup bowls and garnish with chopped chives. Serve immediately.

Pasta and Chickpea Soup

This is a simple, country-style, filling soup. The shape of the pasta and the beans complement one another beautifully.

INGREDIENTS

Serves 4–6

60ml/4 tbsp olive oil

1 onion, finely chopped

2 carrots, finely chopped

2 celery sticks, finely chopped

400g/14oz can chickpeas, rinsed
   and drained

200g/7oz can cannellini beans, rinsed
   and drained

150ml/¼ pint/⅔ cup passata (bottled
   strained tomatoes)

120ml/4fl oz/½ cup water

1.5 litres/2½ pints/6¼ cups vegetable or
   chicken stock

1 sprig of fresh rosemary, plus a few leaves
   to garnish

200g/7oz/scant 2 cups dried conchiglie

salt and freshly ground black pepper

shavings of Parmesan cheese, to serve

1 Heat the oil in a large pan, add the chopped vegetables and cook over a low heat, stirring frequently, for 5–7 minutes.

2 Add the chickpeas and cannellini beans, stir well to mix, then cook for 5 minutes. Stir in the passata and water. Cook, stirring, for 2–3 minutes.

3 Add 475ml/16fl oz/2 cups of the stock, the rosemary sprig and salt and freshly ground black pepper to taste. Bring to the boil, cover, then simmer gently, stirring occasionally, for 1 hour.

VARIATIONS

You can use other pasta shapes, but conchiglie are ideal because they scoop up the chickpeas and beans. If you like, crush 1–2 garlic cloves and cook them with the vegetables.

4 Pour in the remaining stock, add the pasta and bring to the boil. Lower the heat and simmer for 7–8 minutes (or according to the instructions on the packet), until the pasta is *al dente*. Remove the rosemary sprig. Serve the soup sprinkled with rosemary leaves and Parmesan shavings.

Wild Mushroom Soup

Wild mushrooms are expensive. Dried porcini have an intense flavour, so only a small quantity is needed. Beef stock may seem strange in a vegetable soup, but it helps to strengthen the earthy flavour.

INGREDIENTS

Serves 4

25g/1oz/2 cups dried porcini mushrooms

250ml/8fl oz/1 cup warm water

30ml/2 tbsp olive oil

15g/½oz/1 tbsp butter

2 leeks, finely sliced

2 shallots, roughly chopped

1 garlic clove, roughly chopped

225g/8oz fresh wild mushrooms

1.2 litres/2 pints/5 cups beef stock

2.5ml/½ tsp dried thyme

150ml/¼ pint/⅔ cup double
   (heavy) cream

salt and freshly ground black pepper

sprigs of fresh thyme, to garnish

3 Chop or slice the fresh mushrooms and add to the pan. Stir over a medium heat for a few minutes until they begin to soften. Pour in the beef stock and bring to the boil. Add the porcini, soaking liquid, dried thyme and salt and pepper. Lower the heat, half-cover the pan and simmer gently for 30 minutes, stirring occasionally.

4 Pour about three-quarters of the soup into a food processor or blender and process until smooth. Return to the soup remaining in the pan, stir in the cream and heat through. Check the consistency, adding more stock or water if the soup is too thick. Adjust the seasoning. Serve immediately, garnished with sprigs of fresh thyme.

1 Put the dried porcini in a bowl, add the warm water and leave to soak for 20–30 minutes. Lift the porcini out of the liquid and squeeze to remove as much of the soaking liquid as possible. Strain all the liquid and reserve to use later. Finely chop the porcini.

2 Heat the oil and butter in a large pan until foaming. Add the leeks, shallots and garlic and cook gently for about 5 minutes, stirring frequently, until softened but not coloured.

Mushroom and Bread Soup with Parsley

Thickened with bread, this rich mushroom soup will warm you up on cold winter days. It makes a terrific hearty lunch.

INGREDIENTS

Serves 8

75g/3oz/6 tbsp unsalted (sweet) butter

900g/2lb field (portabello)
   mushrooms, sliced

2 onions, roughly chopped

600ml/1 pint/2½ cups milk

8 slices white bread

60ml/4 tbsp chopped fresh parsley

300ml/½ pint/1¼ cups double
   (heavy) cream

salt and freshly ground black pepper

1 Melt the butter and sauté the sliced mushrooms and chopped onions for about 10 minutes until soft but not browned. Add the milk.

2 Tear the bread into pieces, drop them into the soup and leave to soak for 15 minutes. Purée the soup and return it to the pan. Add 45ml/3 tbsp of the parsley, the cream and seasoning. Reheat, without boiling. Serve garnished with the remaining parsley.

Wonton Soup

In China, wonton soup is served as a snack, or dim sum, rather than as a soup course during a large meal.

INGREDIENTS

INGREDIENTS

Serves 4

175g/6oz pork, roughly chopped

50g/2oz peeled prawns (shrimp), finely chopped

5ml/1 tsp light brown sugar

15ml/1 tbsp Chinese rice wine or dry sherry

15ml/1 tbsp light soy sauce

5ml/1 tsp finely chopped spring onions (scallions), plus extra to garnish

5ml/1 tsp finely chopped fresh root ginger

24 ready-made wonton skins

about 750ml/1¼ pints/3 cups stock

15ml/1 tbsp light soy sauce

1 In a bowl, thoroughly mix the chopped pork and prawns with the sugar, rice wine or sherry, soy sauce, spring onions and ginger. Set aside for 25–30 minutes for the flavours to blend.

2 Place about 5ml/1 tsp of the pork mixture in the centre of each wonton skin.

3 Wet the edges of each filled wonton skin with a little water and press them together with your fingers to seal. Fold each wonton parcel over.

4 To cook, bring the stock to a rolling boil in a wok, add the wontons and cook for 4–5 minutes. Season with the soy sauce and add the spring onions.

5 Transfer to individual soup bowls and serve.

Summer Minestrone

V

This brightly coloured, fresh-tasting soup makes the most of seasonal summer vegetables.

INGREDIENTS

Serves 4

45ml/3 tbsp olive oil

1 large onion, finely chopped

15ml/1 tbsp sun-dried tomato purée (paste)

450g/1lb ripe Italian plum tomatoes, peeled and finely chopped

225g/8oz green courgettes (zucchini), trimmed and roughly chopped

225g/8oz yellow courgettes (zucchini), trimmed and roughly chopped

3 waxy new potatoes, diced

2 garlic cloves, crushed

about 1.2 litres/2 pints/5 cups vegetable stock or water

60ml/4 tbsp shredded fresh basil

50g/2oz/⅔ cup grated Parmesan cheese

salt and freshly ground black pepper

1 Heat the oil in a large pan, add the onion and cook gently for about 5 minutes, stirring constantly, until softened.

2 Stir in the sun-dried tomato purée, chopped tomatoes, courgettes, diced potatoes and garlic. Mix well and cook gently for 10 minutes, uncovered, shaking the pan frequently to stop the vegetables sticking to the base.

3 Pour in the stock or water. Bring to the boil, lower the heat, half-cover the pan and simmer gently for 15 minutes or until the vegetables are just tender. Add more stock if necessary.

4 Remove the pan from the heat and stir in the basil and half the cheese. Taste and adjust the seasoning. Serve hot, sprinkled with the remaining cheese.

Apple Soup

A delicious soup that makes the most of freshly-picked apples.

INGREDIENTS

Serves 6

45ml/3 tbsp oil

1 kohlrabi, diced

3 carrots, diced

2 celery sticks, diced

1 green (bell) pepper, seeded and diced

2 tomatoes, diced

2 litres/3½ pints/9 cups chicken stock

6 large green apples

45ml/3 tbsp plain (all-purpose) flour

150ml/¼ pint/⅔ cup double (heavy) cream

15ml/1 tbsp granulated sugar

30–45ml/2–3 tbsp lemon juice

salt and freshly ground black pepper

lemon wedges and crusty bread, to serve

1 Heat the oil in a large pan. Add the kohlrabi, carrots, celery, green pepper and tomatoes and cook for 5–6 minutes until just softened.

2 Pour in the chicken stock, bring to the boil, then reduce the heat and simmer for about 45 minutes.

3 Meanwhile, peel and core the apples, then chop into small cubes. Add to the pan and simmer for a further 15 minutes.

4 In a bowl, mix together the flour and cream, then pour slowly into the soup, stirring well, and bring to the boil. Add the sugar and lemon juice before seasoning. Serve immediately with lemon wedges and crusty bread.

V

Hungarian Sour Cherry Soup

Particularly popular in summer, this fruit soup is typical of Hungarian cooking. The recipe makes good use of plump, sour cherries. Fruit soups are thickened with flour, and a touch of salt is added to help bring out the flavour of the cold soup.

INGREDIENTS

Serves 4

15ml/1 tbsp plain (all-purpose) flour

120ml/4fl oz/½ cup sour cream

a generous pinch of salt

5ml/1 tsp caster (superfine) sugar

225g/8oz/l½ cups fresh sour or morello
 cherries, pitted

900ml/l½ pints/3¾ cups water

50g/2oz/¼ cup granulated sugar

1 In a bowl, blend the flour with the sour cream until completely smooth, then add the salt and caster sugar.

2 Put the cherries in a pan with the water and granulated sugar. Gently poach for about 10 minutes.

3 Remove from the heat and set aside 30ml/2 tbsp of the cooking liquid as a garnish. Stir another 30ml/2 tbsp of the cherry liquid into the flour and sour cream mixture, then pour this on to the cherries.

4 Return to the heat. Bring to the boil, then simmer gently for 5–6 minutes.

5 Remove from the heat, cover with clear film (plastic wrap) and leave to cool. Add extra salt if necessary. Serve with the reserved cooking liquid swirled in.

Star-gazer Vegetable Soup

V

If you have the time, it is worth making your own stock – either vegetable or, if preferred, chicken or fish – for this recipe.

INGREDIENTS

Serves 4

1 yellow (bell) pepper

2 large courgettes (zucchini)

2 large carrots

1 kohlrabi

900ml/1½ pints/3¾ cups well-flavoured
    vegetable stock

50g/2oz rice vermicelli

salt and freshly ground black pepper

1 Cut the pepper into quarters, removing the seeds and core. Cut the courgettes and carrots lengthways into 5mm/¼in slices and slice the kohlrabi into 5mm/¼in rounds.

2 Using tiny pastry cutters, stamp out shapes from the vegetables or use a very sharp knife to cut the sliced vegetables into stars and other decorative shapes.

COOK'S TIP
~

Sauté the leftover vegetable pieces in a little oil and mix with cooked brown rice to make a tasty risotto.

3 Place the vegetables and stock in a pan and simmer for 10 minutes, until the vegetables are tender. Season to taste with salt and pepper.

4 Meanwhile, place the vermicelli in a bowl, cover with boiling water and set aside for 4 minutes. Drain, then divide among four warmed soup bowls. Ladle over the soup and serve.

Pear and Watercress Soup

This unusual soup combines sweet pears with slightly sharp watercress. A more traditional partner, Stilton cheese, appears in the form of crisp croûtons.

INGREDIENTS

Serves 6

1 bunch of watercress

4 medium pears, sliced

900ml/1½ pints/3¾ cups chicken stock, preferably home-made

120ml/4fl oz/½ cup double (heavy) cream

juice of 1 lime

salt and freshly ground black pepper

For the Stilton croûtons

25g/1oz/2 tbsp butter

15ml/1 tbsp olive oil

200g/7oz/3 cups cubed stale bread

115g/4oz/1 cup Stilton cheese, chopped

1 Place two-thirds of the watercress leaves and all the stalks in a pan with the pears, stock and a little seasoning. Simmer for about 15–20 minutes.

2 Reserving some of the watercress leaves for the garnish, add the rest to the soup and immediately blend in a food processor until smooth.

3 Put the mixture into a bowl and stir in the cream and the lime juice to mix the flavours thoroughly. Season again to taste. Pour all the soup back into the pan and reheat, stirring gently, until warmed through.

4 To make the Stilton croûtons, melt the butter and oil and fry the cubes of bread until golden brown. Drain on kitchen paper. Put the cheese on top and heat under a hot grill (broiler) until melted and bubbling.

5 Pour the soup into warmed bowls. Divide the croûtons and reserved watercress among the bowls and serve.

Broccoli, Anchovy and Pasta Soup

This soup is from Apulia in the south of Italy, where anchovies and broccoli are often used together.

INGREDIENTS

Serves 4

30ml/2 tbsp olive oil

1 small onion, finely chopped

1 garlic clove, finely chopped

¼–⅓ fresh red chilli, seeded and finely chopped

2 canned anchovy fillets, drained

200ml/7fl oz/scant 1 cup passata (bottled strained tomatoes)

45ml/3 tbsp dry white wine

1.2 litres/2 pints/5 cups vegetable stock

300g/11oz/2 cups broccoli florets

200g/7oz/1¾ cups orecchiette

salt and freshly ground black pepper

grated Pecorino cheese, to serve

1 Heat the oil in a large pan. Add the onion, garlic, chilli and anchovies and cook over a low heat, stirring all the time, for 5–6 minutes.

2 Add the passata and wine, with salt and pepper to taste. Bring to the boil, cover the pan, then cook over a low heat, stirring occasionally, for 12–15 minutes.

3 Pour in the stock. Bring to the boil, then add the broccoli and simmer for about 5 minutes. Add the pasta and bring back to the boil, stirring. Simmer for 7–8 minutes or according to the instructions on the packet, stirring frequently, until the pasta is *al dente*.

4 Taste and adjust the seasoning. Serve hot in individual warmed bowls. Hand round the grated Pecorino cheese separately.

Consommé with Agnolotti

Prawns (shrimp), crab and chicken jostle for the upper hand in this rich and satisfying consommé.

INGREDIENTS

Serves 4–6

75g/3oz cooked peeled prawns (shrimp)
75g/3oz canned crab meat, drained
5ml/1 tsp finely grated fresh root ginger
15ml/l tbsp fresh white breadcrumbs
5ml/l tsp light soy sauce
1 spring onion (scallion), finely chopped
1 garlic clove, crushed
1 egg white, beaten
400g/14oz can chicken consommé
30ml/2 tbsp sherry or vermouth
salt and freshly ground black pepper

For the Basic Pasta Dough

200g/7oz/1¾ cups plain (all-purpose) flour
pinch of salt
2 eggs
10ml/2 tsp cold water

For the garnish

50g/2oz cooked peeled prawns (shrimp)
fresh coriander leaves (cilantro)

1 To make the pasta, sift the flour and salt on to a clean work surface and make a well in the centre with your hand.

2 Put the eggs and water into the well. Using a fork, beat the eggs gently together, then gradually draw in the flour from the sides, to make a thick paste.

3 When the mixture becomes too stiff to use a fork, use your hands to mix to a firm dough. Knead the dough for about 5 minutes until smooth. Wrap in clear film (plastic wrap) to prevent it from drying out and leave to rest for 20–30 minutes.

4 Meanwhile, put the prawns, crab meat, ginger, breadcrumbs, soy sauce, spring onion, garlic and seasoning into a food processor or blender and process until smooth.

5 Once the pasta has rested, roll it into thin sheets. Stamp out 32 rounds 5cm/2in in diameter, using a fluted pastry cutter.

6 Place 5ml/1 tsp of the filling in the centre of half the pasta rounds. Brush the edges of each round with egg white and sandwich with a second round on top. Pinch the edges together to stop the filling seeping out.

7 Cook the pasta in a large pan of boiling, salted water for 5 minutes (cook in batches to stop them sticking together). Remove and drop into a bowl of cold water for 5 seconds before placing on a tray. (You can make these pasta shapes a day in advance. Cover and store in the refrigerator.)

8 Heat the consommé in a pan with the sherry or vermouth. Add the cooked pasta shapes and simmer for 1–2 minutes.

9 Serve the pasta in soup bowls covered with hot consommé. Garnish with peeled prawns and coriander leaves.

Oyster Soup

Oysters make a delicious soup that is really special.

INGREDIENTS

Serves 6

475ml/16fl oz/2 cups milk

475ml/16fl oz/2 cups single (light) cream

1.2 litres/2 pints/5 cups shucked oysters, drained, with their liquor reserved

a pinch of paprika

25g/1oz/2 tbsp butter

salt and freshly ground black pepper

15ml/1 tbsp chopped fresh parsley, to garnish

1 Combine the milk, single cream, and oyster liquor in a heavy pan.

2 Heat the mixture over medium heat until small bubbles appear around the edge of the pan, being careful not to allow it to boil. Reduce the heat to low and add the oysters.

3 Cook, stirring occasionally, until the oysters plump up and their edges begin to curl. Add the paprika and season to taste.

4 Meanwhile, warm six soup plates or bowls. Cut the butter into six pieces and put one piece in each bowl.

5 Ladle in the oyster soup and sprinkle with chopped parsley. Serve immediately.

Asparagus Soup with Crab

A beautiful, green soup with the pure taste of fresh asparagus. The crab is added at the last moment as a luxurious garnish.

INGREDIENTS

Serves 6–8

1.5kg/3–3½lb fresh asparagus

25g/1oz/2 tbsp butter

1.5 litres/2½ pints/6¼ cups chicken stock

30ml/2 tbsp cornflour (cornstarch)

30–45ml/2–3 tbsp cold water

120ml/4fl oz/½ cup whipping cream

salt and freshly ground black pepper

175–200g/6–7oz white crab meat,
   to garnish

1 Trim the woody ends from the bottom of the asparagus spears and cut the spears into 2.5cm/1in pieces.

2 Melt the butter in a heavy pan or flameproof casserole over a medium-high heat. Add the asparagus and cook for 5–6 minutes, stirring frequently, until it is bright green, but not browned.

3 Add the stock and bring to the boil over a high heat, skimming off any foam that rises to the surface. Simmer over a medium heat for 3–5 minutes until the asparagus is tender, yet crisp. Reserve 12–16 of the asparagus tips for the garnish. Season the soup, cover and continue cooking for 15–20 minutes until the asparagus is very tender.

4 Purée the soup in a blender or food processor and pass the mixture through the fine blade of a food mill back into the pan. Return the soup to the boil over a medium-high heat. Blend the cornflour with the water and whisk into the boiling soup to thicken, then stir in the cream. Adjust the seasoning.

5 To serve, ladle the soup into bowls and top each with a spoonful of the crab meat and a few of the reserved asparagus tips.

Fish and Shellfish Wonton Soup

This is a variation on the popular wonton soup that is traditionally prepared using pork.

INGREDIENTS

Serves 4

50g/2oz raw tiger prawns (jumbo shrimp)
50g/2oz queen scallops
75g/3oz skinless cod fillet, roughly
    chopped
15ml/1 tbsp finely chopped fresh chives
5ml/1 tsp dry sherry
1 small egg white, lightly beaten
2.5ml/½ tsp sesame oil
1.5ml/¼ tsp salt
large pinch of ground white pepper
20 wonton wrappers
2 cos (romaine) lettuce leaves, shredded
900ml/1½ pints/3¾ cups fish stock
fresh coriander (cilantro) leaves and garlic
    chives, to garnish

1 Peel and devein the prawns. Rinse, dry on kitchen paper and cut into small pieces.

2 Rinse and dry the scallops. Chop them into small pieces the same size as the prawns.

3 Place the cod in a food processor and process until a paste is formed. Scrape into a bowl and stir in the prawns, scallops, chives, sherry, egg white, sesame oil, salt and pepper. Mix well, cover and leave in a cool place to marinate for 20 minutes.

4 Make the wontons. Place 5ml/1 tsp of the fish and shellfish filling in the centre of a wonton wrapper, then bring the corners together to meet at the top. Twist them together to enclose the filling. Fill the remaining wonton wrappers in the same way. Tie with a fresh chive if desired.

COOK'S TIP

The filled wonton wrappers can be made ahead, then frozen for several weeks and cooked straight from the freezer.

5 Bring a large pan of water to the boil. Carefully drop in the wontons. When the water returns to the boil, lower the heat and simmer gently for 5 minutes or until the wontons float to the surface. Drain the wontons and divide them among four heated soup bowls.

6 Add a portion of lettuce to each bowl. Bring the fish stock to the boil. Ladle it on top of the lettuce and garnish each portion with coriander leaves and garlic chives. Serve immediately.

Lobster Bisque

The blue and black clawed lobster is known as the king of the shellfish. When cooked, it turns brilliant red in colour. This is an extravagant soup, worthy of a celebration dinner party.

INGREDIENTS

Serves 4

1 cooked lobster (about 675g/1½lb)

30ml/2 tbsp vegetable oil

115g/4oz/½ cup butter

2 shallots, finely chopped

juice of ½ lemon

45ml/3 tbsp brandy

1 bay leaf

1 sprig of fresh parsley, plus extra
  to garnish

1 blade of mace

1.2 litres/2 pints/5 cups fish stock

40g/1½oz/3 tbsp plain (all-purpose) flour

45ml/3 tbsp double (heavy) cream

salt and freshly ground black pepper

a pinch of cayenne pepper, to garnish

1 Preheat the oven to 180°C/ 350°F/Gas 4. Lay the lobster out flat and split in half lengthways. Remove and discard the little stomach sac from the head, the thread-like intestine and the coral (if any).

2 In a large, heavy roasting tin (pan), heat the oil with 25g/1oz/2 tbsp of the butter. Sauté the lobster, flesh-side down, for 5 minutes. Add the shallots, lemon juice and brandy, then cook in the oven for 15 minutes.

3 Remove the lobster meat from the shell. Place the shell and the juices in a large pan and simmer with the bay leaf, parsley, mace and stock for 30 minutes. Strain. Finely chop 15ml/1 tbsp of the lobster meat. Process the rest with 40g/1½oz/3 tbsp of the butter.

4 Melt the remaining butter, add the flour and cook gently for 30 seconds. Add the stock gradually and bring to the boil, stirring constantly. Stir in the processed meat, the cream and season with salt and freshly ground black pepper.

5 Ladle into individual serving dishes and garnish with chopped lobster, parsley sprigs and a sprinkling of cayenne.

Saffron Mussel Soup

This is one of France's most delicious shellfish soups. For everyday eating, the French would normally serve all the mussels in their shells. Serve with plenty of French bread.

INGREDIENTS

Serves 4–6

40g/1½oz/3 tbsp unsalted (sweet) butter

8 shallots, finely chopped

bouquet garni

5ml/1 tsp black peppercorns

350ml/12fl oz/1½ cups dry white wine

1kg/2¼lb mussels, scrubbed
    and debearded

2 medium leeks, trimmed and
    finely chopped

1 fennel bulb, finely chopped

1 carrot, finely chopped

several saffron threads

1 litre/1¾ pints/4 cups fish or
    chicken stock

30–45ml/2–3 tbsp cornflour (cornstarch),
    blended with 45ml/3 tbsp cold water

120ml/4fl oz/½ cup whipping cream

1 medium tomato, peeled, seeded and
    finely chopped

30ml/2 tbsp Pernod (optional)

salt and freshly ground black pepper

1 In a large, heavy pan, melt half the butter over a medium-high heat. Add half the shallots and cook for 1–2 minutes until softened but not coloured. Add the bouquet garni, peppercorns and white wine and bring to the boil. Add the mussels, cover tightly and cook over a high heat for 3–5 minutes, shaking the pan from time to time, until the mussels have opened.

2 With a slotted spoon, transfer the mussels to a bowl. Strain the cooking liquid through a muslin- (cheesecloth-) lined sieve and reserve.

3 Pull open the shells and remove most of the mussels. Discard any closed mussels.

4 Melt the remaining butter over a medium heat. Add the remaining shallots and cook for 1–2 minutes. Add the leeks, fennel, carrot and saffron and cook for 3–5 minutes.

5 Stir in the reserved cooking liquid, bring to the boil and cook for 5 minutes until the vegetables are tender and the liquid is slightly reduced. Add the stock and bring to the boil, skimming any foam that rises to the surface. Season with salt, if needed, and black pepper and cook for a further 5 minutes.

6 Stir the blended cornflour into the soup. Simmer for 2–3 minutes until the soup is slightly thickened, then add the cream, mussels and chopped tomato. Stir in the Pernod, if using, cook for 1–2 minutes until hot, then serve immediately.

Thai Fish Soup

Thai fish sauce, or nam pla, *is rich in B vitamins and is used extensively in Thai cooking. It is available at Thai or Indonesian shops and good supermarkets.*

INGREDIENTS

Serves 4

350g/12oz raw large prawns (shrimp)

15ml/1 tbsp groundnut (peanut) oil

1.2 litres/2 pints/5 cups well-flavoured
  chicken or fish stock

1 lemon grass stalk, bruised and cut into
  2.5cm/1in lengths

2 kaffir lime leaves, torn into pieces

juice and finely grated rind of 1 lime

1/2 fresh green chilli, seeded and
  finely sliced

4 scallops

24 mussels, scrubbed

115g/4oz monkfish fillet, cut into
  2cm/3/4in chunks

10ml/2 tsp Thai fish sauce (nam pla)

For the garnish

1 kaffir lime leaf, shredded

1/2 fresh red chilli, finely sliced

1 Peel the prawns, reserving the shells, and remove the black vein running along their backs.

2 Heat the oil in a pan and cook the prawn shells until pink. Add the stock, lemon grass, lime leaves, lime rind and green chilli. Bring to the boil, simmer for 20 minutes, then strain through a sieve, reserving the liquid.

3 Prepare the scallops by cutting them in half, leaving the corals attached to one half.

4 Return the stock to a clean pan, add the prawns, mussels, monkfish and scallops and cook for 3 minutes. Remove from the heat and add the lime juice and Thai fish sauce (nam pla).

5 Serve garnished with the shredded lime leaf and finely sliced red chilli.

Prawn and Egg-knot Soup

An unusual and special soup, just right for a festive occasion.

INGREDIENTS

Serves 4

900ml/1½ pints/3¾ cups kombu and
    bonito stock or instant dashi
5ml/1 tsp soy sauce
a dash of sake or dry white wine
salt
1 spring onion (scallion), finely sliced,
    to garnish

For the prawn (shrimp) shinjo balls
200g/7oz raw large prawns (shrimp),
    shelled, thawed if frozen
65g/2½oz cod fillet, skinned
5ml/1 tsp egg white
5ml/1 tsp sake or dry white wine
22.5ml/4½ tsp cornflour (cornstarch) or
    potato starch
2–3 drops of soy sauce

For the omelette
1 egg, beaten
a dash of mirin
oil, for frying

1 Devein the prawns. Process the prawns, cod, egg white, 5ml/1 tsp sake or wine, cornflour or potato starch, soy sauce and a pinch of salt in a food processor or blender to make a sticky paste. Alternatively, finely chop the prawns and cod, crush them with the knife's blade and then pound them well in a mortar with a pestle, before adding the remaining ingredients.

2 Shape the mixture into four balls and steam them for 10 minutes over a high heat. Meanwhile, soak the spring onion for the garnish in cold water for 5 minutes, then drain.

3 To make the omelette, mix the egg with a pinch of salt and the mirin. Heat a little oil in a frying pan and pour in the egg, tilting the pan to coat it evenly. When the egg has set, turn the omelette over and cook for 30 seconds. Leave to cool.

4 Cut the omelette into long strips about 2cm/¾in wide. Knot each strip once, place in a sieve and rinse with hot water to remove excess oil. Bring the stock or dashi to the boil and add the soy sauce, a pinch of salt and a dash of sake or wine. Divide the prawn balls and the egg knots among four bowls. Pour in the soup, sprinkle with the spring onion and serve.

Corn and Crab Bisque

This is a Louisiana classic, which is certainly luxurious enough for a dinner party and is therefore well worth the extra time required to prepare the fresh crab. The crab shells, together with the corn cobs, from which the kernels are stripped, make a fine-flavoured stock.

INGREDIENTS

Serves 8

4 large corn cobs

2 bay leaves

1 cooked crab (about 1kg/2¼lb)

25g/1oz/2 tbsp butter

30ml/2 tbsp plain (all-purpose) flour

300ml/½ pint/1¼ cups whipping cream

6 spring onions (scallions), shredded

a pinch of cayenne pepper

salt and freshly ground black and
   white pepper

hot French bread or grissini breadsticks,
   to serve

1 Pull away the husks and silk from the cobs of corn and strip off the kernels.

2 Keep the kernels on one side and put the stripped cobs into a deep pan or flameproof casserole with 3 litres/5 pints/12½ cups cold water, the bay leaves and 10ml/ 2 tsp salt. Bring to the boil and leave to simmer while you prepare the crab.

3 Pull away the two flaps between the big claws of the crab, stand it on its "nose", where the flaps were, and bang down firmly with the heel of your hand on the rounded end.

4 Separate the crab from its top shell, keeping the shell.

5 Push out the crab's mouth and its abdominal sac immediately below the mouth, and discard.

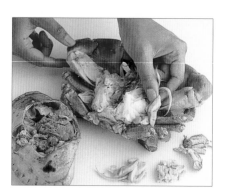

6 Pull away the feathery gills surrounding the central chamber and discard. Scrape out all the semi-liquid brown meat from the shell and set aside.

7 Crack the claws in as many places as necessary to extract all the white meat. Pick out the white meat from the fragile cavities in the central body of the crab. Set aside all the crab meat, brown and white. Put the spidery legs, back shell and all the other pieces of shell into the pan with the corn cobs. Simmer for a further 15 minutes, then strain the stock into a clean pan and boil hard to reduce to 2 litres/3½ pints/9 cups.

8 Meanwhile, melt the butter in a small pan and sprinkle in the flour. Stir constantly over a low heat until the roux is the colour of rich cream.

9 Remove from the heat and slowly stir in 250ml/8fl oz/ 1 cup of the stock. Return to the heat and stir until it thickens, then stir this thickened mixture into the pan of strained stock.

10 Add the corn kernels, return to the boil and simmer for 5 minutes.

11 Add the crab meat, cream and spring onions and season with cayenne, salt and pepper (preferably a mixture of black and white). Return to the boil and simmer for a further 2 minutes. Serve with hot French bread or grissini breadsticks.

Seafarer's Stew

Any variety of firm fish may be used in this recipe, but be sure to use smoked haddock as well; it is essential for its distinctive flavour.

INGREDIENTS

Serves 4

225g/8oz undyed smoked haddock fillet

225g/8oz fresh monkfish fillet

20 mussels, scrubbed

2 streaky (fatty) bacon rashers (strips) (optional)

15ml/1 tbsp olive oil

1 shallot, finely chopped

225g/8oz carrots, coarsely grated

150ml/¼ pint/⅔ cup single (light) or double (heavy) cream

115g/4oz cooked peeled prawns (shrimp)

salt and freshly ground black pepper

30ml/2 tbsp chopped fresh parsley, to garnish

1 In a large, heavy pan, simmer the haddock and monkfish in 1.2 litres/2 pints/5 cups water for 5 minutes, then add the mussels and cover the pan with a lid.

2 Cook for a further 5 minutes or until all the mussels have opened. Discard any that have not. Drain, reserving the liquid. Return the liquid to the rinsed pan and set aside.

3 Flake the haddock coarsely, removing any skin and bones, then cut the monkfish into large chunks. Cut the bacon, if using, into thin strips.

4 Heat the oil in a heavy frying pan and cook the shallot and bacon for 3–4 minutes or until the shallot is soft and the bacon lightly browned. Add to the strained fish broth, bring to the boil, then add the grated carrots and cook for 10 minutes.

5 Stir in the cream together with the haddock, monkfish, mussels and prawns and heat gently, without boiling. Season and serve in large bowls, garnished with parsley.

Pasta Soup with Chicken Livers

A soup that can be served as a first or main course. The fried chicken livers are so delicious that, even if you do not normally like them, you will find yourself lapping them up in this soup.

INGREDIENTS

Serves 4–6

115g/4oz/½ cup chicken livers, thawed
   if frozen
15ml/1 tbsp olive oil
a knob (pat) of butter
4 garlic cloves, crushed
3 sprigs each of fresh parsley, marjoram
   and sage, chopped
1 sprig of fresh thyme, chopped
5–6 fresh basil leaves, chopped
15–30ml/1–2 tbsp dry white wine
2 x 300g/11oz cans condensed
   chicken consommé
225g/8oz/2 cups frozen peas
50g/2oz/½ cup small pasta shapes
2–3 spring onions (scallions),
   sliced diagonally
salt and freshly ground black pepper

1 Cut the chicken livers into small pieces with scissors. Heat the oil and butter in a frying pan, add the garlic and herbs, with salt and ground black pepper to taste, and cook gently for a few minutes. Add the livers, increase the heat to high and stir-fry for a few minutes until they change colour and become dry. Add the wine, cook until it evaporates, then remove from the heat.

2 Tip both cans of chicken consommé into a large pan and add water to the condensed soup as directed on the labels. Add an extra can of water, then stir in a little salt and pepper to taste and bring to the boil.

3 Add the frozen peas to the pan and simmer for about 5 minutes, then add the small pasta shapes and bring the soup back to the boil, stirring. Allow to simmer, stirring frequently, for about 5 minutes or according to the instructions on the packet, until the pasta is *al dente*.

4 Add the fried chicken livers and spring onions and heat through for 2–3 minutes. Taste and adjust the seasoning. Serve hot, in warmed bowls.

Ginger, Chicken and Coconut Soup

This aromatic soup is rich with coconut milk and intensely flavoured with galangal, lemon grass and kaffir lime leaves.

INGREDIENTS

Serves 4–6

750ml/1¼ pints/3 cups coconut milk

475ml/16fl oz/2 cups chicken stock

4 lemon grass stalks, bruised and chopped

2.5 cm/1 in piece galangal, finely sliced

10 black peppercorns, crushed

10 kaffir lime leaves, torn

300g/11oz skinless boneless chicken, cut into thin strips

115g/4oz button (white) mushrooms

50g/2oz/½ cup baby corn

60ml/4 tbsp lime juice

45ml/3 tbsp Thai fish sauce (nam pla)

For the garnish

2 red chillies, chopped

3–4 spring onions (scallions), chopped

chopped fresh coriander (cilantro)

1 Bring the coconut milk and chicken stock to the boil in a pan. Add the lemon grass, galangal, peppercorns and half the kaffir lime leaves, reduce the heat and simmer gently for 10 minutes.

2 Strain the stock into a clean pan. Return to the heat, then add the chicken, mushrooms and baby corn. Cook for about 5–7 minutes until the chicken is cooked through.

3 Stir in the lime juice, Thai fish sauce (nam pla) to taste and the rest of the lime leaves. Serve hot, garnished with red chillies, spring onions and coriander.

Indian Beef and Berry Soup

The fresh berries give this soup a pleasant kick.

INGREDIENTS

Serves 4

30ml/2 tbsp vegetable oil

450g/1lb tender beef steak

2 medium onions, finely sliced

25g/1oz/2 tbsp butter

1 litre/1¾ pints/4 cups good beef stock
or bouillon

2.5ml/½ tsp salt

115g/4oz/1 cup fresh huckleberries, blue-
berries or blackberries, lightly mashed

15ml/1 tbsp honey

1 Heat the oil in a heavy-based pan until almost smoking. Add the steak and brown on both sides over a medium-high heat. Remove the steak from the pan and set aside.

2 Reduce the heat to low and add the sliced onions and butter to the pan. Stir well, scraping up the meat juices. Cook over a low heat for 8–10 minutes until the onions are softened.

3 Add the beef stock or bouillon and salt and bring to the boil, stirring well. Mix in the mashed berries and the honey. Simmer for 20 minutes.

4 Meanwhile, cut the steak into thin, bitesize slivers. Taste the soup and add more salt or honey if necessary. Add the steak to the pan. Cook gently for 30 seconds, stirring constantly, then serve.

Index